Anne,
Munsy

Little

Remember me to K. A.!

Other Books by David Spanier published by Oldcastle Books
Easy Money
Total Poker

DAVID SPANIER

♠♥♣♠♦♠♥♣♦♠♠♥♣♦

The Little Book

of Poker

OLDCASTLE BOOKS

First published in Great Britain by Oldcastle Books Ltd

This edition published in 1999 by Oldcastle Books,
18 Coleswood Road, Harpenden, Herts, AL5 1EQ.

http://www.highstakes.co.uk

A CIP catalogue record for this book is available
from the British Library.

ISBN 1 901982-54-8   The Little Book of Poker

2 4 6 8 10 9 7 5 3 1

Typeset in Scala by Koinonia, Manchester
and printed and bound in Great Britain by
Caledonian International Book Manufacturing, Glasgow.

Contents

(1)
Intro

Do you have a secret lifetime's ambition? Some people want to climb Mount Everest or sail around the world single-handed. My own dream was more modest, though still quite difficult to realize. I wanted to write a poker column in a national newspaper.

In the summer of 1993, I made it. And what's more, in my favourite paper, *The Independent*. I suggested the idea, after writing a book review on gambling, and the managing editor (what a guy!) said, 'OK, give it a shot.' I remember driving back home down the grey City Road as if I were floating on a cloud.

So far as I know, mine was the first and (may be still is) only poker column in a national daily, here or in America. Anyway, it seemed a nice idea, five years later, to re-print some of my efforts. I begin with my first column, from July 1993, and present a selection of others arranged according to themes.

(2)

How to win and lose a million

A three-handed duel in the saloon settled the 1993 world poker championships in Las Vegas.

At the final table at Binion's Horseshoe Casino, John Bonetti and Jim Bechtel each had around $1m in chips in front of them. A third player, Glenn Cozen, had 'only' $100,000.

The stakes go hysterically high in the final round, because they represent the sum of the stakes of the original 220 contestants, a total of $2.2m, busted over the previous three days' play. First prize in the championships looks a tad cumbersome: an even million in hundred note bills is stacked up on the table.

What is the right strategy in this three-handed duel? Is the outcome going to be decided by luck, or a huge bluff, or by remorselessly grinding the opponents down? None of these. What decided the championship was a principle which underlines all poker games, of whatever size: money management. Obviously the two players with all the money should just wait for the third man to go broke, as he is bound to do with antes and openers costing about $20,000 each deal. They can then square up to each other, head to head, for first place. But that is not what happened.

Bonetti was dealt ace-king off suit, which at Texas Hold 'em is a very strong hand. Hold 'em is a faster form of seven card stud stud, now the most popular form of poker out West. Each player is dealt a hand of two cards, face down, followed by five cards face up in common, as follows:

(xx)   **xxx**   **x**   **x**
hole cards / the 'flop / 'the turn' / 'the river'
opening   bet   bet   bet
   bets

It looks a simple game, but in fact the play can be as subtle as chess (if rather more expensive). Playing on about $800,000, Bechtel bet $20,000 as an opener, which both Cozen and Bonetti called. Obviously all three have playable hands. The flop came king-6-4, with two spades. Bonetti and Cozen checked to Bechtel who bet $70,000, and Bonetti then put in a check raise.

For Cozen to call this bet would take all his remaining chips. Far better for him to sit back and watch the action. If one of the two big money players knocks the other one out, Cozen will automatically take second place in the championship, despite being down to his last few chips. So he folded. Jim Bechtel merely called the raise.

Bonetti: **Ah Kd**   Bechtel: **(? ?)**
Flop: **Ks 6s 4h**

What can Bechtel have? A king with a lower kicker is no use. A 6 and a 4 is not credible as a starting hand. A flush draw, or a draw to hit a low straight, would be prohibitively long odds at these stakes.

Fourth up-card, however, showed the jack of spades. And here, apparently with no thought at all, Bonetti, in a flashy gesture, shoved all his remaining chips – some $500,000 – into the pot. The crowd roared.

His huge 'all-in' bet signified he had hit a spade flush.

Bechtel, who is a cotton farmer from Arizona when not playing cards, and a pretty steady fellow, thought for a minute, and called. 'I put him on two kings,' Bechtel said afterwards. 'I didn't want to lose him by raising him on the flop. The jack of spades was a danger card for me, but if he had made a flush, he would have just bet $100,000 or so.'

Bechtel showed two sixes in the hole, giving him three sixes. No matter what the fifth and final up-card might be, his opponent was dead in the water. Another king, for instance, giving Bonetti trip kings, would make Bechtel a full house. The pot was worth $1,387,000 in chips.

Bonetti is renowned as an old pro but his reckless bet was a terrible misjudgement of the money situation. If he thought Bechtel was weak, why push him out? The right play was to test him with a feeler bet of say, half the pot, and see what happens. This move cost him $200,000 in cash, the difference between coming third in the championship, as he did, or taking at least second place.

As for Cozen, he couldn't believe his good fortune. Two minutes later, he was out. He had won $400,000 by sitting tight at the crucial moment.

Bonetti's rush of blood, when he was so close to glory, and a first prize of $1m., was described as the worst play in the world championships.

Personal

(3)

Sam's Night Out

It is bound to be an emotional night – your 17-year-old son's first foray into a cash game. He knew all about Hold 'em, of course. But his previous experience of poker was limited to jolly games round the kitchen table with school-friends. The boy started well – almost too well. Every time he had A-x in the hole he raised and took the pot unseen, or out-ranked a weak caller. The game was played in an open, friendly, jocular spirit, but it was for real money. 50p. from the dealer, 50p. small blind and £1 from the opener.

The trouble with winning early on is that your luck is sure to cool off. Late into the session, the boy as dealer, found **A-J** in the hole, and raised, correctly, £5. He got a caller from the small blind, who was a solid player, and also the big blind, a gamesome lady pushing her luck. Down came the flop: **K-Q-7**.

The boy checked. The solid player bet an unemotional £15. The lady hesitated and called. The boy also called. This was his first mistake: he should have asked himself the question: what has the solid player got? Whatever it is, it can hardly be less than a king in the hole. The lady, in her flighty way, could be playing on anything or nothing. Next card was another king, making a pair on board.

The boy checked and Mr. Solid bet another careful £15. The lady only had £15 left and reluctantly put it in. Now the boy more or less knew he was beaten, but convinced himself that the odds of catching an inside straight justified a call. And as if by magic, down came a 10 on the river, just like that.

(A-J) K-Q-7 K 10

Unperturbed, Mr. Solid bet another £15. The boy called the £15 and set himself in for his remaining £12. Alas and alack, his straight was no good. He had in fact been drawing dead, because Mr. Solid had **K-Q** in the hole, for an unbeatable full house. The poignancy of this clash was that Mr. Solid was the boy's father, me.

"No tears," remarked the son on the way home. "It had to happen."

(4)

New Year Resolutions

Let me make my New Year's Resolution perfectly clear, as Richard Nixon might have said. I shall not play poker when drunk, tired, emotional, or otherwise out of sorts, or when the opposition round the table seems too tough, too rich, too dodgy or otherwise disagreable. I break this precept all the time – to my cost. On the other hand, if you only played poker when in complete control, when would you ever play?

A couple of years ago I proffered a trio of good resolutions, which are instructive to review in the cold light of experience. (1) Set a limit.

This point is elementary. If you set a limit on how much you are prepared to lose, or can afford to lose on any given night, you avoid disasters, financial or emotional. This applies, of course, to all and every kind of gambling.

(2) Hang on to your winnings. If things are going your way, the temptation is to let the upside rip. What I meant to imply was: Don't be greedy. Better to stash part of your winnings before your luck turns around. Some punters get the idea when they are playing up winnings that they are on a free roll, gambling with *their* (the bookies' or other people's) money. Not so: they are playing with their *own* money. Better follow the Rothschild maxim: No one ever went broke taking a profit.

(3) The most important New Year's resolution is to stay in control and to understand what you are doing. I

score about half on that one. I must confess to the occasional lapse. Not so much going on tilt as dwelling on mistakes. I don't gamble, but I do tend to make big wagers – say, on seats won and lost at the general election – in the spirit of a convivial night out, which as a matter of honour I can't get out of, or even remember very clearly the following morning.

At poker, self-control is the most important quality of all. It implies concentration, card sense, courage, judgement and money management. Can you combine all these talents after a Saturday night binge, or a crisis at the office or a family row? You bet you can!

(5)

Boys will be Boys

Just for fun, half a dozen 18-year-old kids came round for a game of poker the other night. They wanted to find out what poker was all about.

We were a merry group. One young man wore a white stetson, another sported a green eyeshade and brought his own bottle of bourbon. I threw a green baize over the kitchen table and set the stakes at 5p. a chip. The game chosen, of course, was Texas Hold 'em, with one chip for the small blind and two for for the big blind.

You can learn the rules of poker in about five minutes. But how long does it take to learn to play? "All your life, son," was playwright Michael Pertwee's classic answer. And he was right, because the game is a continuous learning process. For the first few rounds, the betting was cautious. One chip bets and two chips raises was about as high as it got, and if someone hit a pair, however small, there was no shaking him out of the pot.

The boys bought in for £5 worth of chips each. First man out, with an ace in the hole, refused to believe that with two jacks and an ace on the flop, his opponent could possibly have a third jack. He raised and re-raised until all his money was gone, to discover that the other fellow did not, indeed, have three jacks. He had four.

Next man out was unlucky. Dealt a pair of 7s in the hole, the flop came 2-8-Q. He felt pretty sure he was best and bet his hand up. But the next two up-cards were another 8-Q, making two higher pairs on board than his pocket 7s. His own pair, therefore, was completely valueless. Unfortunately he did not realize what had happened, and went right on betting.

As the bourbon went down, so the adrenalin went up. The action really got going, with all sorts of big bets – 20p and raise you 20p – and freakish out-draws. In one five-handed deal, four players were dealt pairs in the hole, each one declaring himself a winner at the end – 5s, 9s, kings and finally aces.

In the last round, gambling fever bubbled over and the stakes were raised to 25p ante and 50p blind. One man with A-6 thought he was done for when the flop came Q-J-10, but as by that stage all his chips were in, he did not have to take any further action in the pot. Sure enough, a king popped up on the last card to give him a top straight.

In the last hand, the player with all the chips found himself betting on a pair of 4s as if there was no tomorrow. Last card brought a 5, which paired his opponent, who had been playing 5-6 in the hole. Funny old game, poker.

As the guys filed out, long after midnight, one question remained: "Hey, who's giving the game next week?"

(6)

Loads

One moment in poker games I have come to dread. It is when a friend or acquaintance sidles up behind my chair and whispers: 'Dave, can I have a quick word?' I know in advance what he's going to say and even how much he is going to ask for. But it's almost impossible to get away, despite the warning precept which invariably comes to mind: 'Neither a lender nor a borrower be.'

Certainly it is best to say no, quickly and politely, with the rider that you just never do it. In practice, life is not so simple. First of all, you know the guy. Second, you more or less sympathise with his plight. And third, most important, you probably need him there to help keep the game going. In poker games, everyone has a pretty shrewd idea of everyone's financial situation: who is a millionaire underneath his denim shirt, and who is playing for his rent money underneath his Armani suit. The loan must be judged accordingly.

In one game I played in, we had a safety net, whereby everyone took a piece of a loan or shared a bad debt, collectively. This meant that when the worst came to the worst, as occasionally it did, the loss was shared by everyone alike. That is a good plan which cannot, unfortunately, be extended to public card rooms. Most players in casinos borrow from each other as a matter of routine. It is understood by both sides that the borrower is waiting to hit a lucky streak before even thinking of repaying the lender. And even then, it is not so easy.

One man I know eventually got his money back by playing a little trick of his own. He asked the borrower, in the middle of a big game, for change of a thousand-pound chip. When the player had counted it down, the man swiped it off the table and slipped away, smartish.

Even in Vegas, or perhaps especially in Vegas, where the top players gamble for colossal sums on the golf course or on football games, there is an endless network of borrowing. One of the (slightly pernicious) services offered by American casinos is cash machines in the gaming area. This practice now extends to British casinos. So how do you decline a loan? Just say no.

Women

(7)

Battle of the Sexes

Women are no longer considered accessories to be brought to the poker table, but as equals at the game. One of the best of them is June Field, editor of the magazine *Card Player*.

At a recent testimonial honouring her editorial achievement, held at the Bicycle Club – a vast poker palace close to Los Angeles – June recalled that her aim had been to give poker a positive image, to erase its 'negative, back-room, cigar-smoking stigma'.

However, there is not much danger of that happening, I am glad to say. Poker will always keep its low-life glitter, because of its image of daring and danger. Cowboy movies have instilled the saloon-bar image of poker as a man's game. Now that women are considered equals at the poker table, the only criterion is a talent to play.

I once put forward the theory that as poker depends on the swashbuckling 'masculine' attributes of courage, aggression and bluff, it followed that women who assumed such qualities would, to that extent, be denying their 'femininity'. I was assailed as a fogey and heretic for advancing such a sexist view.

It is obvious that women can be as tough as men at the table and retain or revert to their essential nature away from the game. This is not to say that sex cannot enter poker. A woman at the table can alter the chemistry of the game. All is fair in love and cards.

If a woman can exploit her sexuality by a certain

smile, a look, a little flirting, to put a male opponent off his game, she is entitled to do so. Any man who responds, in the spirit of the occasion, should be even more on his guard. The object on both sides (one must assume) is to win the pot.

The original first lady of poker was in fact an Englishwoman, Alice Ivers, born in 1851, who became known in the mining camps of Colorado as Poker Alice. A female player in those days wore long skirts and always managed to look ladylike.

Alice, however, took the precaution of packing a Colt .45, and could use it if she had to. Asked if she ever lost much, Alice gave a sharp reply: 'I never seen anyone grow humpbacked carrying away the money they won from me' – delivered in a clipped British accent.

Playing in a small game not long ago at Laughlin, in the southern tip of Nevada on the Colorado river, I found myself seated next to a gamesome lady – seventy years old if she was a day – berating her luck that she could not catch a pair of aces.

I offered her the trite old poker saw: 'You've got to live right to get aces, Ma'am.' She looked at me over her spectacles: 'Then I guess I'm never gonna git 'em.'

Poker is not a man's game any more. It's a person's game.

(8)
Oh Maria!

When Maria Stern won the $1,500 seven card stud tournament at the World Series of Poker at Binion's this year it seemed like a victory for all women poker players. Then it turned out that she had made a deal with the second placed player, whereby she took the winner's gold bracelet, in return for his taking a bigger share of the prize money. This devalued her victory more than somewhat, even though she played well to get so far and might have won the title legitimately, had she played it out.

So when Ms. Stern was interviewed in *Card Player* recently, I expected to read some explanation or justification for her action.

Instead I read: "I believe in destiny. I think there is a cause and effect for everything in life. Sometimes you may ask, 'Why is this happening to me? I don't deserve it.' It's not a question of deserve or not deserve, it is a question of karma."

To which one might reply: making deals about the result of a world series tournament is very bad karma. Deals about sharing out the prize money among the final players are fair enough, and indeed commonplace, provided they are openly arrived at. Deals about winning a world title devalue the result and are unworthy of the players. Such action is against the spirit of the game.

Certainly it is very important that tournaments are played out, and seen to be played out, fairly. This is something which British card rooms need to watch. If the final two or three players in contention choose to make a deal and divide the prize money, that is fair enough. The arrangement should be made openly, at the table, in front of any other contestant concerned.

In a tournament at a Midands casino recently, a London poker player complained at "blatant collusion" between local players, who were not betting into each other at the final table. He was told there was nothing which the dealers or supervisors could do about it. Why not? If anyone has any practical suggestions, drop me a line at *The Independent*. Meanwhile the Association of European Poker Players is taking up the issue, to try and establish clear rules of conduct.

One Mistake

One mistake is all it takes to be knocked out of a tournament. It is especially painful when a player has steered through long hours of struggle and is, at last, in sight of the final table. One player who will think long and hard (as all losers do) of how she misplayed a crucial hand is Barbara Samuelson, rated as one of the strongest woman players on the pro circuit.

It was no limit Hold 'em, the third night of the World Championship.

Ms. Samuelson found a pair of deuces in the hole. She raised and got one caller. Hugh Vincent, a retired accountant from Florida, was a player previously unknown in Las Vegas. He had been playing pretty solidly. Out came the flop:

B: (2♣ 2♦)
Flop 3♣ 4♦ 5♦
H: (? ?)

Both players checked. Next card off was the 6♦, giving Barbara a straight. What is the right play here? Certainly a bet is in order. It would obviously be a mistake to give her opponent a free draw at a flush, if he happened to hold a high diamond. If he has nothing, he will fold right away. If by some unlucky chance he had two diamonds, say A-x and raises her back, she can think again, and fold. The question was: could he have a higher straight? He would hardly have called a pre-flop raise on a bare 7-x in the hole, one of the least promising hands at hold 'em.

So Barbara decided to go for it. She pushed forward the stacks of chips she had accumulated through the previous three days of the tournament and went all in. The dealer counted them down, $167,000. The spectators craning around the table held their breath. Without fuss, her opponent moved his own chips forward to call. And as is the practice when the money is all in, both players turned over their hole cards.

He also had a straight, but two pips higher 4♦-5♦-6♦ with the 7♦ 8♠ – not an unreasonable starting hand. Barbara was done for. No last up-card could save her. Any diamond loses, including the 3d which would have given her a straight flush!

If Barbara Samuelson had won this pot, she would have made history by becoming the first woman ever to reach the final table of the world championship. She did well in reaching 10th place, with a consolation prize. Her day will come:

"I'm here to win it, not to act sweet," she told the table. Her conqueror finished in second place, winning $588,000 – the cad.

(10)

Lucy's Way

Agal's gotta do, what a gal's gotta do. So it was with Lucy Rokach, the Stoke-on-Trent poker player and recent Las Vegas winner, when she came up against Mickey Finn, last year's European champion. The event was the no-limit Hold 'em tournament at the Grosvenor Victoria earlier this week.

On the small blind, Lucy found an interesting sort of hand, A♦-3♥ and bet it. Mickey on the button called. Down came a potentially exciting flop, 6♣-7♦-8♦, threatening a straight. Lucy checked and Mickey checked. Now came a 6♦, making a flush draw and a pair on board.

L (A♦ 3♥) 6♣-7♦-8♦ 6♦
M (? ?)

It was mid-way through the tournament and no one had more than a few thousand chips. Lucy checked again, and Mickey made a very small, feeler sort of bet, 1,000 units.

This was a like the scent of fresh blood to a tigress. Lucy immediately raised him 3,000. Without a moment's pause, Mickey moved the rest of his chips to the centre, another 4,000. It was obvious that a player of his calibre had a strong hand – but Lucy had no hesitation in calling. As Mickey was all-in, the cards were turned face up.

He showed a 10-9 in the hole, for the top straight.

But on the river, down came another diamond, to give Lucy the nut flush and the pot.

To me, watching the action, it looked like an outrageous out-draw, but Lucy explained it differently. "There was no way I was going to give up that hand, after putting so many chips into the pot. At first I thought he was bluffing, then I realized he had a hand. But I knew that if I hit my flush, I was going to win a lot of chips. The point was, even if I missed it, I still had another two or three thousand left to fight my way back."

Mickey took his defeat gracefully. Perhaps he realized that at that stage of a tournament it is better to amass a stack of chips than try fancy plays. He was unlucky to lose on a straight, but in tournament play luck goes around. Lucy eventually took third prize, a consolation £5,370, after being outdrawn in the final.

Loving Couples

Some people think gambling is a substitute for sex. It is probably more correct to say that while the two activities do not go together, one may follow the other. What also seems true is that loving couples do not make good partners at the poker table. Too much is at stake, either in affection or rivalry. But here is an exception.

Akio, a high rolling Japanese player, decided he wanted to take a quick drink at the bar and deputed his girlfriend to take his seat. This was a medium-size game of Hold 'em, and she knew, sort of, how to play.

First hand the lady was dealt **A-Q** suited, and raised, rightly so. Her opponent, who was an experienced player, had 9-9 in the hole. And as luck would have it, the flop came down 10-9-7, off-suit, which was about as good as it could be for him. The Japanese lady bet the pot and naturally he raised her. Her A-Q looked okay to her and she called.

(A-Q)
Flop 7 9 10
(9-9)

Next card off was a king, and again she bet, presumably on some kind of bluff. Her opponent, who had put her on ace-ten or perhaps ace-king, rather than a high pair, raised her back some £350.

At this point, Akio returned, having had a quick scotch on the rocks.

He saw, to his evident amazement, that the huge pile of chips he had been playing on was now being stacked up by the dealer, in the centre of the table. He sat down behind his companion and peeked at her hole cards. Of course he was not allowed to say anything. There was no need for him to utter a word. The lady had no hesitation. In went the rest of her – or his – money.

Akio's inscrutable smile rapidly faded into a scrutable frown. The dealer turned the river card. It was a jack. She had hit a back-door (last two cards) straight. The trip 9s were busted. The Japanese gentleman showed no emotion as the money was pushed over and he resumed his seat. The moral of this story is: sometimes it pays to drink and play.

World Championship

(12)

The Big One

By the time you read this, my fate will be sealed. This year (1997), I am playing in the big one – the World Championship of Poker at Binion's Horseshoe in Las Vegas. For any poker player, this is a lifetime's dream, which in my case has been realized by the generosity of a poker playing friend, who is backing me in raising the $10,000 entry fee – what a pal!

I have about as much chance of winning the event, which is no-limit Texas Hold 'em, as of beating Tiger Woods at golf. But that is not the point. What counts is the thrill and experience of competing against so many great players, including a whole raft of world champions. What's more anyone can get lucky, which in this event means catching a few good hands at the right moment.

"You may be a 100 to 1 shot," the enthusiastic and talented Vegas pro Annie Duke encouraged me, "but that means that once in 100 times you're gonna win!"

I have seen too many friends crash in the World Championship to have any such illusions. One year, a player went out in the very first hand – he hit four aces and came up against a straight flush! No disgrace, but so painful. My fellow poker writer Al Alvarez got trapped on a pair of queens early on when he played, and Tony Holden had aces wired outdrawn by a lucky flush to finish in 111th place. "I reeled away badly winded," he recalls in *Big Deal*, "as if I'd been punched hard in the stomach – a real physical pain, gradually giving way to a deep spiritual bruise."

My objective is a modest one. I want to survive the first session and if possible the first day. I intend to follow a policy of "selective aggression", ie. playing very few hands but playing them hard, as recommended by Tom McEvoy in *Tournament Poker*. I may crash out, but I intend to give it my best shot. If I get through to the second day, that would be time enough to consider my game plan. Fortunately there is a ready cure for being busted – move over to a new game as fast as possible.

Ben's Bad Beat

London player Ben Roberts was the unluckiest player in the World Poker Championship, despite taking home $150,000 for his sixth place finish. The event, as usual, was played at Binion's Horseshoe in Las Vegas last week, with a record field of 350 – which at $10,000 per entry produced a prize fund of $3.5m. With aces in the hole, Roberts contrived to get all his chips in the pot against Scotty Nguyen, who had only ace-jack of diamonds, and Swedish player Jan Lundberg on a pair of 10s. Roberts was a huge favourite to win a three-way pot worth $350,000. But on the last card, Nguyen caught a deuce of diamonds to make a flush.

He went on to win the tournament and become the new world champion. (Last year's winner and pre-tournament favourite Stu Ungar was unfortunately unable to play due to his perennial health problem.)

Iranian-born Roberts displayed admirable British sangfroid in congratulating the lucky winner, who was whooping his triumph all over the room. "These things happen, it's all part of the game," Roberts observed mildly, adding: "I enjoyed the experience of playing in the tournament very much."

35-year-old Nguyen (his name, happily, is pronounced 'win'), a former refugee from South Vietnam, clinched the title in a hard fought duel against Kevin McBride, a management consultant from Florida, who only got involved in tournament play a few months ago. In what turned out to be the final hand, Nguyen found

J♦-9♣ in the hole. The flop came down 8♣-9♦-9♥ giving him trips. McBride had Q♥-10♥ giving him an inside straight draw with a jack.

The fourth card was 8♥ giving Nguyen a full house. and McBride two pairs with a queen kicker. Nguyen made a light bet, to lure his opponent on, in the hope he might catch a flush or a straight on the river. Last card was 8♠, making a full house on the board. Nguyen now put his opponent all in. McBride thought he was simply trying to steal the pot. In any case he was too far committed to back down and called for the rest of his chips. The pot was worth $1.2m.

Mc Bride: Q♥ 10♥   Nguyen: J♦ 9♣
Flop: 8♣ 9♦ 9♥ 8♥ 8♠

"Remember this hand, baby!" exulted the winner, waving a bottle of beer in one hand and a huge stack of dollar bills in the other. Wasn't he just a bit worried about the possibiity of four 8s out against him? "I didn't even think about it, baby!" Consolation for the runner-up was a prize of $687,500. I saw the new champion the next afternoon, mooching about in a green tee-shirt, looking for a game. He didn't look any different from the other guys.

(14)

Al's Fiasco

Poet and novelist Al Alvarez drank deep from the cup of misery on Monday. For a year he had been looking forward to playing in the World Poker Championship. Not many poker players can turn their hand to poetry. But every poet worth his rhymes longs to take on the top players of the world in his chosen sport in Las Vegas.

Within three hours of the first deal, Alvarez was busted in 232nd place. No disgrace in that. Three former world champions bit the dust before him, as the laws of chance turned against them.

So it was with Alvarez, playing Texas Hold 'em, which is the game of the World Championship. He was dealt two queens in the hole, and with some $7,000 in chips in front of him, raised the opening bet. One player called and immediately re-raised.

Alvarez called – in the heat of battle, a man can hardly be expected to put down queens back-to-back. Even so, on the opening of the World Championship, when everyone plays very tightly in order to survive, a re-raise should have been a warning.

Out came the flop, with a king on board. His opponent set Alvarez in for his remaining chips, which were by then only $1,000 or so. There was really no choice. Alvarez called the final bet only to discover ace-king in his opponent's hand, outranking his own pair of queens.

Afterwards friends and supporters gathered round

to console the hapless loser, telling him that he had done the right thing. But like so many others in this cruel game, luck had deserted him when he most needed it.

As Alvarez himself admitted, there is a 'quantum leap' between the ability of British and American players. In his heart he knew this, but in the moment of decision, it proved sadly all too true.

Mansour Matloubi, the only British player to win the World Championship, explained that a pair of queens is a dreadfully difficult hand to play – too strong to throw away and too weak to go all-in on. 'When I got queens in the hole tonight, I threw my hand in. I might have been wrong, but I'm so happy to have survived to fight again tomorrow.

Other British players fared quite well in the first day's play. Best placed is Surinder Sunar of Wolver-hampton on $25,600, followed by Matloubi on $15,275 and Colin Kennedy, hanging in on $7,000. In a record field of 268 entrants, the winner will be the player who knocks out all the other competitors to win the $1m. first prize.

Al's Revenge

Al Alvarez, poet and poker author, waited a year to take his revenge on the player who busted him out of the World Poker Championship, when he was last in Las Vegas. This time round, Alvarez played his hand to perfection, to despatch his former opponent. The irony was that the player involved, Billy Baxter, renowned as the biggest sports bettor in town, had not the faintest recollection of his previous victory over Alvarez, which had hurt him so deeply. To the professional poker players, the past is gone and each deal is a new hand.

The event this time was a $2,500 entry, no-limit Hold 'em tournament. Al, sitting after the blinds (first to speak), was dealt A♠ 4♠. He raised and Baxter called. Out flopped a red ace and two spades. Alvarez kept calm and checked. Baxter bet, Al just called. Next card off was a 4. Now Alvarez, with aces-up, was virtually certain he was best, but wanted to trap his man. He checked, Baxter bet out, and Al again flat called. Last card was another spade.

Alvarez: (A♠ 4♠)
Flop: A♥ 10♠ 6♠ 4♣ 7♠.
Baxter: (? ?)

Now Al ventured a small bet, as if to try and steal the pot. Baxter raised, obviously putting his man on aces-up. And Al, sitting on a cinch, went all in. To his surprise, Baxter called him. Al showed his ace flush.

His opponent threw his cards in, pushed his chair back and quit the table. Later, he said he also had a flush, presumably a high one. This was good, risk-free play by Alvarez. He could well have raised on fourth street, but did not want to face a re-raise if by some outside chance his opponent had concealed trips.

Seed is Rich

'**S**mile! You're rich!' screamed the photographers. Huck Seed, 27, who had just won the World Poker Championship at Binion's Horseshoe Casino in Las Vegas and was, notionally, $1,000,000 better off, managed a faint smile in return. He seemed a modest young man. He was also, by general consent, the best player in the 1996 championship, who deserved to overcome his 294 rivals. He will bring a fresh face – wholesome as his name – to high stakes poker.

The final hand of the championship was a real Hold 'em hand and not, as so often, a crap shoot. The blinds (antes) were $10,000 and $20,000. Huck led off with a small raise, his challenger, 57-year-old pathologist Dr Bruce Van Horn from Oklahoma, raised him back, and Huck went all in. When the Doc called, it became the biggest pot in world championship history, totalling $2,328,000.

Seed: ♦9–♦8
Van Horn: ♣K–♣8
Flop: ♥9 ♠8 ♣4

With two pairs, Seed was obviously a big favourite. But the turn card showed ♣A.

This gave the Doc the chance to draw out on the river by catching a flush, as well as a king for two higher pairs. Seed's sleepy country-boy look, bred from his early days in Montana, was unchanged, but I saw a pulse throb in his cheek.

The dealer turned the last card: ♠3

In fact the players were competing at this stage only for the title. A little earlier, the last three players, who included veteran John Bonetti, had done a deal to split the prize money $680,000 to each man. This safety precaution, which is normal in tournament poker, ensures the finalists all get a good whack, while sparing the eventual loser the pain of a (relatively) small pay-out, from what might be just a stoke of bad luck at the end.

The title of World Champion, however, is priceless. Seed, 6ft 6in in his shorts and sneakers, worn without socks, gave up college to play poker. His four brothers and sisters are university educatcd. It seems safe to say he will make more money at cards than the rest of the family put together.

Stu Again

S tu 'the Kid' Ungar won the World Championship at Binion's Horseshoe in Las Vegas last week, and won it easily. He earned his nickname from winning back-to-back titles in 1980 and again in 1981, when still in his twenties. Now aged 43, looking like a little dried-up mannikin in blue-tinted glasses, he has done it a third time – a unique sporting achievement. The years in between his titles, as he explains, he spent in various forms of self-indulgence which took him away from poker. Now he is back.*

Stu's quality, according to the experts, is that he continually gives his opponents heat. He has an uncanny ability to read no-limit Hold 'em, which enables him to keep the pressure on through every deal. For instance, I saw him call a $90,000 bet to win a good pot holding only a king high, and then run a queen-jack to force another opponent to give up pocket nines. His post-victory comment did not sound immodest: 'No one has ever beaten me at cards, I have only beaten myself.' As for gin rummy, he has long been considered the best in the USA.

In the final hand, Stu got lucky. Heads up against John Strzemp, president of Treasure Island hotel-casino, Stu had a $2,385,000 to $735,000 lead. He opened for $60,000 on ♥A–♣4. His opponent called with ♠A–♣8. At this stage a bare ace is a powerhouse, so they were both correct. Down came ♣A–♦5–♥3 on the flop. Strzemp bet $120,000 and Ungar put him all-in for just over half a million more, to make a $1,940,000 pot. They then flipped over their cards for the cameras. The turn card was another three, giving Strzemp the lead with his eight kicker.

Ungar: (♥A–♣4)
♣A–♦5–♥3–♠3
Strzemp: (♠A–♣8)

Stu was underdog, but not by all that much. He needed a deuce or a four to win outright, but any card higher than an eight would have been a split pot. The river brought a deuce to make Stu's gut–shot straight. You could say he was lucky, but in most onlookers' judgement he would have still won the title had he missed. My own exploits I shall relate next week.

* Stu Ungar died 22 November 1998.

(18)

Exit Dave

I returned to London after playing in the World Championship at Binion's Horseshoe in Las Vegas very much richer. Richer, that is, in experience rather then greenbacks. Everyone should enter the event once in their lives. The championship is an intense emotional experience because everyone involved – this year there were 312 entrants paying $10,000 each – knows it is the biggest deal in poker. Fourteen former world champions were competing and an array of top class American and international players.

What can I tell you? I lasted until almost the end of the first day, by which time 150 entrants had been busted out. I played badly, mainly in not pushing my good hands hard enough. If the eventual winner, Stu Ungar, had had my cards, I have no doubt he would been $10,000 ahead, rather than $10,000 down, on the first night.

The physical drive of the event is relentless. On the first day we played four two-hour sessions, with a fifteen minute break between them, which is only just long enough to make it to the loo. On the second day, when the field was reduced to 27, the players were in action for over twelve hours. One slip is enough to ruin your chances.

When a player is busted, he simply stands up and quits the table. No one looks up, no one has time to commiserate. He or she feels simply terrible, but that is the downside of competing. After a day or two, the shock and the pain wear off. Hey! At the end of the championship 300 or so other players all feel bad, too. 'Bad beat city' is my nickname for Las Vegas.

Here is my final hand. Sitting on the little blind, everyone folded round to me. I found J-J wired. I decided to try and double through on my remaining $5,000 in chips, and checked to the big blind. (I should have bet, to win the antes, not give him a free draw!)

Down came what I thought was a dream flop: 10-8-7, giving me a higher pair plus a gutshot straight draw. I bet my stack and after some thought he called. He showed 10-8, which stood up. *Exit Dave.*

Tournaments

Tournament Poker

The popularity of poker tournaments prompts the question: what makes a good tournament? I should explain, first of all, what a tournament is, which explains in turn why players like them so much. In tournament poker (as distinct from cash games) each player pays an entry fee to buy chips.

All of the money all goes into a prize pool which, in the end, is divided among the winners – sometimes the last 4 or 5 to survive, sometimes the final table.

So if 100 players put up £50 each, the pool is £5,000. In fact, the total prize money would normally be substantially higher, say £8,000, thanks to 'buy-ins', when players who get knocked out early take another shot at it. If first place pays 50%, the winner would take home £4,000; second place might be 25%, third place 10%, and so on. The attraction is two-fold: the chance of a high prize for a small outlay, plus the fun of competing against all kinds of players – masters and minnows alike.

According to former world champion Tom McEvoy, writing in *Card Player*, any event which promises 50 times or more your original buy-in is a good tournament. He, of course, makes his living from playing in tournaments across the U.S. and expects to get into the money more often than not. For new players, I would advise that any tournament where most of the entrants look like they are going in for the fun of it is worth going for. You need a lot of experience to learn how to survive in tournaments – simply because when you have lost all your chips, you are O-U-T. But as in most things in life, you have to pay to learn.

Here is a strange incident I saw in a no-limit Hold 'em satellite, when McEvoy mis-read the hands. He was all-in with **A-K** against another man with **A-Q**. The flop came down **A-10-A-10-Q**. The hole cards were turned, each man had an ace to make a house, so the dealer split the pot. A couple of hands later, when it was all over, McEvoy's opponent suddenly yelled: "Hey! I had ace-queen in that hand!" To his credit, McEvoy pushed over all his chips and quit the table.

(20)

Aces in Trouble

A large number of hard luck or bad beat stories concern the best hand you can catch at Hold 'em, which is of course a pair of aces. This hand will stand up most of the time. "No hand will win more pots or more money no matter how many people are in the pot," notes David Sklansky in his definitive booklet on Hold 'em. Because everyone knows this, players tend to go mad on aces and stick all their chips in, regardless. That is bad policy. Aces do lose, some of the time.

The right technique is to raise, or re-raise, a pair of aces against a full table. You need to thin out the opposition, because aces play better heads up (two-handed) as distinct from in a multi-handed pot with open-ended straight or four flush draws against you (which need a large number of opponents to justify the odds.) Obviously if you have only a small amount of chips, you go all in.

But playing in a tournament off a big stack, it is a mistake to commit all you've got before the flop, with the risk of being busted out if it goes wrong. If several players call the raises, it is far more prudent to hold back, and take a look at the flop. Some flops are very bad for aces. For instance, Q-Q-3 has probably made someone trips; likewise 7♦-8♦-10♦ or 10-J-Q look very threatening. If you think your aces are stranded, better to fold and live to fight another day.

Suppose first prize in the tournament is £10,000. Effectively, that is the potential value of your chips which you are risking trying to blast pocket aces, regardless. If two or three players have committed themselves on pre-flop bets, they have got something. Your aces may still be winning. But is it worth risking everything on that chance? If you are outdrawn, hard luck. You can go around telling everyone how it happened. And you have the whole night to think about how you might have played the hand more sensibly.

Winner Take All

You need luck in poker tournaments, because in the nature of this winner-take-all style of play, there will be several occasions when you cannot avoid putting all your money in the pot. You may be a big favourite to win the hand and still be outdrawn. When that happens in a normal game, a player can dig into his pocket for more money. But when you are busted in a tournament, you are left with nothing but a very cold feeling. That is why this style of play is known as "freeze out." Everyone has a hard luck story to tell, but here's a recent example which takes a lot of beating.

It was a Hold 'em tournament. Ali was dealt a pair of 6s in the hole and bet. Big Paddy, an Irish gambler, well known for his exuberant style of betting, raised. Ali, though a cautious man, re-raised, knowing his opponent probably held only an ace and a low side card. Big Paddy immediately re-raised him back again. When the flop came out 6-4-4, Ali felt very happy. He had flopped a full house which looked unbeatable.

Naturally he stuck the rest of his money in. Big Paddy, holding A-Q off-suit, decided to call. He was too far in to back down now and was hoping (mistakenly) that another ace or queen would be enough to do it for him. In tournament play you have to go for it.

Ali: (6 6)
Flop: 6♥ 4♣ 4♦
Paddy: (A Q)

When all the players' chips are in the pot, so there can't be any further betting, the players simply turn over their hole cards, and the dealer completes the hand. Fourth up-card was another 4, which left Ali's full house 6s on 4s intact. Now he was safe – or so he thought. But the final up-card, amazing to relate, was the last 4. There were now four 4s on the table, common to both players. So Big Paddy's lucky ace decided the hand. Bad beat.

(22)

Double Champ

Most people agreed that Dan Harrington was a worthy winner of the no-limit Hold 'em European Championship, staged at the Victoria casino in Edgware Road, London, last weekend. Harrington, from Downey, California, showed himself a master of the game, in all departments. He came to town, more or less exhausted, after lifting the world championship in Las Vegas, worth $1,000,000. Naturally, everyone wanted to take him on. His reward in London was a more modest £68,500.

"I feel that winning these two tournaments back-to-back, was something like Bobby Fischer wiping out his opponents in the candidates matches," a weary but elated Harrington confided. "It was my experience as a chess player which gave me the concentration to play through these events. The strain is intensely physical, more than anything else." At the age of 49, Harrington is the oldest man to win the Las Vegas world championship since the far off days of Johnny Moss, who only had a couple of tables to contend with.

Harrington's quality in London was shown by his never being ruffled, by his continual 'moves' in the game, to take the initiative away from his opponents, by his outplaying everyone at the final table, and giving the impression overall (certainly mistaken by his opponents) that he was a rock-solid player who always had aces or kings in the hole. "Nothing is more important than to know your opponent's opinion of the way you play," he explained.

Harrington does not believe in 'brilliance' at poker. "In the modern game everyone knows the percentages and the correct plays. What marks out the top players is how they handle themselves when they are losing. I do not think any of the European players whom I have seen are world class," he says, adding the quick rider, "*yet*". There are nuances in the game, which the American pros have, he feels, which are not quite developed in play here. It's hard to pin him down on this, in the same way that it is often hard to show exactly why a chess master makes a particular move. Partly it is an ability to handle very high stakes.

The runner-up in the European Championship at the Vic was Mickey Finn, a well known Irish-American player, now resident in Frankfurt. He made one of the greatest comebacks since Lazarus, playing head to head against Harrington. With only a few thousand chips left he went all-in with **10-2** against Harrington's **10-6** and the flop came **6-7-10**.

It looked all over for Finn, but the next card dealt was a **2**, follow by another **2** on the river! Hold 'em is a game of surprises but this was something else. As the impassive (and well named) Mickey Finn re-built his stack, Harrington had to buckle down and win it all over again. When Finn went all in on **K-7** spades he finally caught him with **A-K**. A great finale.

(23)

Frank in Vegas

It is a long way from Saltburn to Las Vegas but Frank Thompson, 42, has never looked back. One of the youngish group of pros on the poker circuit, who divide their play between Vegas and Los Angeles, he scored his first major success by winning the seven card stud high-low split competition in the recent world series at Binion's Horseshoe. First prize was $94,000.

"I'm very surprised," Thompson said, adding with characteristic Yorkshire phlegm: "I'm delighted that I finally got back some of the huge amount of money I've poured into these tournaments over the years."

Thompson's victory, continuing a British tradition of success in the world series, showed true grit. He was down to his last seven chips before the dinner break, which allowed him just two more antes. His first hand when play resumed was no good, of the K–10–6 variety, but then he was dealt a playable hand on the button, which picked up the blinds. In a couple more hands he had moved from zero to $18,000 in chips, and was ready to battle his way through the final table.

When it came down to the last two players, he got lucky, Thompson says. He outdrew Ted Forrest, whom he rates as a better player, when he hit a middle pin straight, after completely misreading his opponent's hand.

If he had missed that draw, Thompson would have been done for. As it was, he scooped the pot and, against all expectation a couple of hours earlier, found himself snapping a tournament winner's gold bracelet round his wrist. Winning an event in the world series (leaving aside the money) is like an initiation rite into the highest circle of poker pros.

It is not an easy life, however. The sums of money won (and lost) are huge. Most of the Vegas pros stake each other, or have a share of each other's winnings, to help ride out dry spells. Most of the pros also have a 'leak', such as gambling on sports, which is like a black hole for a poker player's bankroll. Professionals who live and play as they please, every day, take these ups and downs as the price of freedom.

(24)

Luck of the Irish

The luck of the Irish held up for Aidan Bennett, first ever winner of the new title of European Poker Champion. He eliminated an array of international rivals in the final tournament, held at the Club d'Aviation in Paris last week. A worthy winner, he amply justified the prediction about his talent for the game in the players' auction: "Big occasion player. Aggressive and creative. Took Hold 'em event at the Amsterdam Masters last year. World Series experience. Capable of running over the table. Cannot be ignored."

And so it turned out. Eighteen players joined battle in the final, which was staged in an unusual format: alternate rounds of pot limit seven card stud with no-limit Hold 'em. These are two very different types of game both in pace and style. Hold 'em is a shoot-from-the hip, all-action game. Seizing the initiative is the key to it. Stud requires a more analytical, card-reading approach, because so much more information about the hands is revealed.

"Aidan plays in a lot gears," a friend explained. "He can play in a very easy, jokey way. Or he can stare down an opponent and frighten him half to death."

When the final came down to nine players, the game reverted to no-limit Hold 'em only. Three players were left in at the dinner break (which as you would expect in Paris is a serious five course repast): Bennett from Dublin, fellow Irishman Mike Magee who plays in London, and Hungarian Tibor Tolnai, a big winner on the European circuit.

Tolnai made his exit when he tried a 'steal' with **Q-10** and ran into Magee's **A-K**. The heads-up encounter was settled when Bennett went over the top with **8-8** against Magee's **A-9** off-suit – near enough a fifty-fifty chance. There is always an element of luck in these shoot-outs. On the night, it went 37-year-old Bennett's way.

In a few jousts I have had in club games with the champion-to-be, what struck me most strongly was his aggressive betting and devil-take-it attitude when his play went wrong, as it quite often did. I recall in particular a hand of Omaha when it went right for him. I raised with the fabulous hand of **A-A-K-J** and Bennett re-raised on something like **5-7-8-10**, which figures to hit at least something on the flop.

Sure enough, he picked up two small pairs and went all-in. My flush draw (which kept me in) failed to hit and my aces stayed bare. Good players make their own luck.

Faces

(25)

Woody's Hand

In his new movie *Manhattan Murder Mystery*, Woody Allen has a nice little joke about poker. He can't play the game but wants to improve. A lady who has quite different designs on him, played by Anjelica Huston, offers to give him lessons. They sit in a restaurant, she coolly inspecting her hand, cigarette dangling, Woody desperately clutching five cards in front of his specs.

He sorts them furiously, realigns them, shuffles again, resets them, and stares at his hand intently.

The lady waits patiently.

Finally she asks him how many cards he wants to draw.

"Four," says Woody blandly.

(26)

Cruisin'

It doesn't get any better than this!" my dealer observed, gazing out at the baby blue ocean, sipping at her iced daiquiri, as we reclined on the sun deck of our cruise ship. This was just off Grand Cayman Island in the western Caribbean, last November. As I recalled the ace-king flush she had just dealt me against a top straight (bless her), I had to agree. Cruisin' 'n playin' takes a lot of beating.

The idea of a poker cruise is to play cards among a group of fellow enthusiasts, while enjoying a vacation at sea. This cruise attracted a group of 320 players and hangers-on. We embarked from Fort Lauderdale, Florida, made several sunny stop-overs at island resorts, as a refreshing break from all-night poker, sailing back to port a week later. The tour, on a white Holland America liner, 15 decks high like a floating hotel, was arranged by a Las Vegas travel agency run by June Field, founding editor of *Card Player* and a sharp player herself. My voyage cost me around $1,150, sharing a cabin, all on-board expenses included – a bargain.

We played limit raise Hold 'em, seven card stud and Omaha high-low, with daily tournaments to enliven the action. Stakes ranged from $2-$4 up to $10-$20 and $20-$40, American style. A clutch of real gamblers got a pot limit Hold 'em game going in the corner.

The games were not too tough, because a certain shipboard jollity infused all the play. But even at these low stakes, it is easy to lose (or win) several hundred dollars. How did I do? "I paid my expenses," is my story. The dealers, taking a break from their regular jobs in Las Vegas casinos, joined in the spirit of a fun trip. They relied on tips, normally a dollar a hand.

One of the pluses of this kind of cruise is that non-poker playing spouses or companions can also have a good time, snorkelling, sight-seeing or snoozing. Cruise coming up are to Alaska, starting from Vancouver, and the Caribbean, from Fort Lauderdale.

B & F Enterprises, 1751, East Reno Avenue, Las Vegas 89119.

(27)

Randolph Fields

Randolph Fields lit up any poker game he played in. Some players thought he was good value because he threw his chips into the pot with such abandon. Others recognised that beneath this swashbuckling play, Randolph had a pretty sharp mind for cards. I often saw him demolish the table by his aggressive betting in tournaments. Above all he brought a boyish enthusiasm to the game, a zest for a good gamble, which is quite rare these days. His untimely death at the age of 44 last month leaves a seat open which will be hard to fill.

Randolph had another claim to celebrity, beyond his poker. As co-founder of Virgin Atlantic, he sold his share in the company to Richard Branson, in return for a life-time of free travel, first class. This entitled him to fly his friends over to Las Vegas or other resorts, all free of charge, whenever he felt like a new game.

I was the beneficiary of a trip to Foxwoods, the amazing Indian reservation casino in Connecticut, a year ago. Randolph played day and night, chortling over how he managed to terrify the Americans, who were not used to his style of high flying pot limit. Our friendship did not stop Randolph running me out of several hands in the Hold 'em tournament.

He would rake in the chips, grinning: "Knew you didn't want to risk your whole stack on an ace-king, did you?" Randolph would and did. He took his own defeats with the same grace as his wins, which is the highest tribute you can pay any poker player.

In his working life Randolph developed an international consultancy, specializing in remote, marginal or otherwise arcane insurance claims. It was all very technical and far beyond my understanding. What was not in doubt was that he became an acknowledged master of this abstruse branch of the business, feared and respected. It seemed to me like another aspect of his poker game – daring to find value where others would drop out.

Recently he opened a card club on the island of Jersey. His true motive, I felt, was to enable him to play poker closer to home and family, instead of criss-crossing the ocean.

(28)

Mason

I saw a TV programme recently, which showed how a pride of lions will lounge for days around the edge of a herd of antelope until they feel hungry, then always pick on a weak or enfeebled animal for their prey. The image struck me as possibly relevant to poker. "In poker most of the money comes from the bad players," says American author Mason Malmuth (a hunter in a different sense). His statement may seem obvious, but its application is not quite so straightforward.

For example, a game which features mediocre players, says Malmuth, is not nearly as "good" as a game that features a bunch of experts with two really awful players in it, who are almost assured of losing all their money. As a pro, his motivation is not so much cynical as brutally realistic. It is to win money. Leisure, pleasure, fun, he finds (presumably) away from the tables, where he is looking for soft games, and only soft games. He does not particularly enjoy playing against experts at his own level.

"I'm not really interested in matching wits against other great players... I look for the easiest games." The bottom line for Malmuth is not how *well* a few other people may play, it is how *badly* a few people play. If there are enough bad players in the game, even one or two if they really play atrociously (weak prey), it is worth playing, regardless of other strong players.

For this reason Malmuth prefers the California card rooms over Vegas. Because the rake (house cut on each hand) is so high, beginners or novice players cannot survive long enough to learn how to play a decent game. As they drop out, more new players come in, thanks to the large population base (the herd), so the process is continuous. In other sports, he concedes, players want to be evenly matched because it makes the game more enjoyable. That is not, for him, the point of playing poker.

In mitigation I should say that Mason himself is a very agreeable fellow, with a quiet, even under-stated, presence at the table. But I would add, speaking from experience, that it is better to read his works than to sit down with him.

Puggy's Ban

There are some things you cannot do at the poker table. One of them is to hit a dealer. Dealers, by common consent, are a terrible crew who always give you the card you don't want while giving your opponent the one card he does want. Why are dealers like this? It's their nature.

Fortunately, they have a specially toughened skin which enables them to withstand insults, jibes, criticism and complaints, and still somehow keep their sanity and their jobs.

But hitting a dealer goes beyond the bounds of what is permissible behaviour, whoever you are. Which brings me to the sad case of former world champion Puggy Pearson. Pug is a brash, voluble, easy-going fellow, with a voice like a buzz-saw. He won the world championship in 1973 on a single ace in his hand, beating Johnny Moss who had a straight draw.

A year or two back, Puggy was inducted into the Poker Hall of Fame at Binion's Horseshoe. In recent months he has taken to driving across America in an enormous RV (recreational vehicle), which is what the Americans call motorised mobile homes. Painted on Pug's huge van in glowing red is the following challenge, which he likes to vaunt as he drives around:

I'll play any man from any land,
At any game which he can name,
For any amount which I can count.

From his moment of glory in the world championship, everything seemed to go downhill. Pug took up backgammon much more enthusiastically than the game took up him. He found it tough to recover his form at poker. But he enjoyed the life of a celebrity, swaggering around the card games in satin shorts and an open-necked shirt, a row of cigars sticking out of his breast pocket like a missile launcher. Win or lose, Pug always came on strong.

As he would tell you, he had come a l-o-o-ng way from growing up dirt poor in Kentucky, in a family of nine children, when they never had enough to eat. "I started hustlin' real young," Puggy recalls, "at ten or eleven." He will not be hustling any more at the Four Queens in downtown Vegas. Last month he slapped a dealer. Pug has been banned there for life.

Places

(30)

Poker in Paris

The estimable Bruno Fitoussi staged his most successful ever week of poker tournaments at the Aviation Club de France in Paris last week. This elegant establishment, ideally situated at 104, Champs Elysées, is rapidly becoming a home from home for British players.

Door-to-door, via Eurostar, is three hours and a taxi ride. It is a civilised spot – "We always take a break for dinner," Fitoussi explained. "No French poker tournament would ever be played without stopping for le dîner!" Quite right, too – and he has also introduced the excellent facility of non-smoking tables, which even in tournaments can apply at least for the first hour or two. My impression of French players is that they may play less well, but they do behave rather better, than their British counterparts. Play starts at 4pm and goes on until 6 am.

Two variations of Hold 'em and Omaha are played at the Club d'Aviation which are new to British players. *Courchevel* is 5-card Omaha, with the first card of the flop turned face up before the betting. If you hold, for example, **Q-J-9-8-6** and a **10** or a **7** pops up, it would be encouraging. If on the other hand an ace is the exposed card, you might not fancy pushing a hand with a pair of kings in it.

Aviation seems to be a club speciality. It is 4-card Hold 'em, with one discard before the flop, and a second discard after the flop. **A-K-9-8** could be preferable to **A-K-Q-J**, where you might have to throw away cards you need on the flop. This variation is not to the purist's taste, but seems like a good idea to spice up home games.

French and English poker terms are more or less interchangeable in the club but here is a basic glossary: Call = *Suivi*; Raise either *Pot* or state the amount; Straight = *Suite* or *Quinte* ; Flush = *Couleur* ; Full house = *Full* ; Four of a kind = *Carré*. Bonne chance!

Pai Gow at the Bike

The earthquake in Los Angeles, so I am informed, has not destroyed the main highway out to the Bicycle Club. Quite a relief to poker players. 'The Bike' is an immense palace of poker situated a few miles out in a suburb of LA. A noisy, brash, pulsating, comfortless shed, the Bike's attraction is that it features some 300 poker games at any one time, half of them Chinese games.

Pai Gow Poker, the playing card version of the Chinese domino game, is most popular in southern California, where the oriental population is crazy to gamble. If you find yourself in LA one night, with nothing on offer but tortillas and skin flicks, the Bike is the place to be.

Pai Gow Poker is banked by the house. Each player is dealt seven cards, from which he has to make *two* hands – a front hand of two cards and a back hand of five cards. A 52-card deck is used, plus a joker which counts only for aces, straights and flushes. The skill lies in setting these hands, the only rule being that the back hand must be higher than the two-card front hand.

After all the players have set their cards, the banker turns his own two hands over. If you win both, you get paid evens on your stake. If you win one and lose one it is a stand-off. The bank's edge comes from the rule that if the banker ties one of the hands, he wins it. In addition, the bank takes a 5% commission, as in baccarat, on player's winning hands. All in all the bank has about a

5% edge, falling to 2.5% against best play.

However, the attraction of Pai Gow for serious poker players is that you can also run the bank yourself. Smart players will hold the bank as long as possible, because they can then turn the 2.5% edge in their favour, which is a pretty big edge in gambling (about the same as single zero roulette).

The object at Pai Gow, of course, is to win both hands. Strategy runs the gamut between between conservative play (going for safe wins on one hand) and aggressive play (playing for a higher proportion of decisions on both hands). For example if you were dealt four aces, you should split them, rather than play them all in the back hand. If you got dealt a flush (which happens quite often with the joker) a safe but naieve strategy would be to set it in the back hand; a more aggressive strategy, such as the casino banker might play, would be to split the flush if the seven cards also contained two pairs, setting the lower pair in the front hand. The banker's skill lies in reading the other players' strategy.

As Confucius might have said, if Pai Gow is inevitable, relax and enjoy it.

(32)

San Francisco

Forget everything you ever learned about Hold 'em! I have been visiting the card casinos around San Francisco, and I can tell you that the Chinese gamblers who throng these downmarket dives have re-written the game. Don't sit around waiting for aces and kings. What you should be looking for are hands like 5-8 off-suit or 10-2 suited.

In the course of a couple of hours at Ladbroke's card casino in San Pablo, forty minutes north of San Francisco, I saw such hands win monster pots. The game was $6-$12 limit Hold 'em, with blinds of $3-$3-$6. The usual pattern was a couple of $6 raises before the flop, which five or six or even seven players call. "Show me the money!" they scream.

Down comes an indeterminate flop like **6-7-Q**, off - suit, which provokes a furious series of new bets and raises. At this point there is already close to $150 in the pot, which makes it very difficult to fold any sort of hand which is in with a chance, such as bottom pair or a middle pin draw to a straight. The value for a $12 bet, even with a raise, is so good it just can't be turned down.

On the turn, if a blank like a deuce or other unhelpful card falls, the hand may be checked all the way round. But if someone does bet, it is sure to be check-raised. Everyone holds their breath as the river card is dealt. Perhaps it pairs a low card, more likely it makes a possible straight – who knows what's going on. The betting takes off again. Someone has hit a miracle back-door flush (last two flop cards in suit). The man who came in on wired kings or perhaps even hit trip queens on the flop, watches the mountain of chips disappear.

The winner of the pot then proceeds to dominate the game, until someone else outguns him. Of course you can't beat Hold 'em this way, can you? The only counter-measure I can suggest is to take every raise going, when you catch a playable hand, and hope it stands up. One good pot can make up for many losses. Ladbroke's card casino, done in a sort of shocking pink Ali Baba-goes-to-Hollywood style, is a class act. The games are structured to produce high action. Bay 101 in San Jose is also well worth a visit. Under the latest Californian decree, there is no smoking in any public place, including casinos. But beware! It's dangerous enough without the smoke.

Reno on a Roll

Reno is on a roll. 'The greatest little city in the world', as this gambling cross-roads in the north-west of Nevada first billed itself, has long been eclipsed by Las Vegas. Now it has picked itself up thanks to a surprising diversion: ten pin bowling.

Americans' passion for bowling is one of those popular pastimes which go on all over the country without attracting much attention just because it is so ordinary. It was an inspired stroke by Reno city planners to build a national stadium, within bowling distance of the casinos. This high-tech stadium, with 80 bowling lanes (imagine 80 cricket pitches in a line), now hosts the American bowling championships for men and women. It will produce two million room-nights for Reno hotels over the next decade, and add a billion dollars to the local economy.

The centre of Reno contains a cluster of big casinos which blaze out their attractions in a dazzle of glitz and neon. Now in a new development, the casino complex has, literally, crossed the wrong side of the tracks, and moved north. Among the new properties, the new Silver Legacy is among the best designed casinos I have ever seen. In the centre of the gaming floor, a huge replica of a mining shaft chunters away, under a painted sky which changes colour from dawn to dusk. (Silver mining in Nevada these days is only a romantic memory, supplanted by nuclear testing). The Silver Legacy's decor, all glossy wood and shiny brass under multi-colour tiffany lamps, might be described as frontier-modern.

Reno is never going to challenge Vegas. But as a gambling resort four hours drive from San Francisco, and forty minutes from the skiing at Lake Tahoe, it has its own appeal. The poker, however, is not up to much. The games are low-level Hold 'em and seven card stud, which help pass the time for blue-collar retirees and off-duty casino employees.

All the action has moved across to the card rooms of California, where a new arrival is Ladbroke's poker club at San Pablo, just outside San Francisco. This is a big, friendly card room, whose pop-Spanish design makes a piquant contrast with its predominantly Asian clientele. Well worth a visit.

(34)
The Taj

The good news is that Atlantic City is not the grim grunge of a place it once was. It is improving so fast it has become almost agreeable. In fact from the 50th floor of Trump Taj Mahal, looking down at the Atlantic rollers racing into the gleaming casinos curving around the shore, one can believe that the ugly sister of gambling has turned into a princess. In reality, down at sea-level, the Boardwalk is less enticing, certainly in the winter months. But still, Atlantic City is now half way to becoming a resort.

The credit is due in part to the pervasive efforts of Donald Trump. He has not changed his style from (in the words of an associate) a street-sharp New York builder. *ie.* he doesn't really understand casinos as such, although four of his properties dominate the place. He has in a sense re-created Atlantic City in his own image. What all of us poker players can thank the Donald for is the rise of poker at The Taj Mahal.

Last month saw the first so-called American Poker Championship at the Taj, which attracted hundreds of players. There were 90 tables in action! That is a lot of poker: 60 tables in the main card room and an overflow of 30 on the casino floor. Poker is not a big money earner for the Taj: it contributes an insignificant $5m. to an overall annual profit of $140m. But the 'synergy' provided by the card room is regarded as very valuable, in raising the profile of the casino. Likewise, there has been a knock-on effect in stimulating poker at other casinos, notably at Resorts next door.

The atmosphere in the card-room at the Taj Mahal is frenetic – so noisy and crowded and disorganised, indeed, that the staff have to communicate with each other via mobile phones, to pass a message of a seat open. Never mind, this was the first year of the Taj championship and things will get better. The Taj's longer term aim is to challenge Binion's in Las Vegas, by establishing itself as the poker capital of the East Coast. There are an awful lot of truckers and muckers from Philly, doctors and dentists from New York, rarin' to play.

(35)

Only Connecticut

Do you know where you can find over one hundred poker games, ready to go? Just a couple of hours drive from the capital? Not London, of course, but New York. There are 75 tables in operation at Foxwoods and now 39 tables at the Mohegan Sun. These two 'native American' casinos on Indian reservations are located a mere ten miles apart in the greenwoods of Connecticut.

Foxwoods, run by the Mashantucket Pequot tribe, is one of the wonders of the gambling world, the biggest and most succcessful casino in the western hemisphere. The Mohegan Sun is a new arrival, not yet one year old, run by the survivors of the famous 'last of the Mohicans'. It turns out that the Mohegans (modern spelling) were not consigned to oblivion after all. Instead, they have found a new way of life, in partnership with Sol Kerzner, creator of Sun City in South Africa.

It is significant that among the thousands of slot machines both properties have given time and space to poker. The games are mostly low limit, running from $3-$6 and $5-$10 Hold 'em and seven card stud for casual players and tourists, through $10-$20 and $20-$40 for more experienced players, up to high action games at Foxwoods, where the pros and the gamblers like to play $75-$150 and $300-$600 limit. At weekends, the tables are jammed.

As many British players have found to their cost, there is a big difference between limit poker, as played in American card rooms, and pot limit, as played here. At pot limit, one big hand can change everything, making you a fortune if you get lucky or sending you home broke. It is a much more dangerous, trappy and exciting kind of game.

At limit poker, the idea is to make, or to save, one extra bet per hand, and do it again and again. The top players' hourly win rate is about one and a half big bets ($60 at the $20-$40 game) an hour, but of course the fluctuations vary hugely around this mean. Best to start small and work your way up. The attraction of Foxwoods and the Mohegan Sun go well beyond poker. They are located in one of the most beautiful tracts of New England.

(36)

Las Vegas Advice

Las Vegas, as many people know, offers fantastic value. Your dollars may go down at the speed of light at the slots and the tables, but in the hotels and restaurants you can live very well for next to nothing. I can recommend, therefore, a newsletter called the *Las Vegas Advisor*, published monthly by a friend of mine who is a specialist in fringe benefits.

So, for first time in ten years, Binion's Horseshoe late-night steak dinner has dropped out of the top 10 list. It used to cost an amazing two bucks, then it was raised to three, and now it has gone up to four dollars. I think it is still unbeatable value, but the *Advisor* disagrees. It rates the show at the newly built Stratosphere as the best value in town. Despite its high-rise thrills, the elegant Stratosphere is failing to draw the crowds because of its terrible location in mid-town.

Nevertheless, for the price of two drinks, the *Advisor* rates its showroom as the best deal currently on offer.

Best buffet is listed as the Texas Station downtown. Its prices start at $3.95. The usual buffet style in Vegas is you can help yourself to as much as you can eat, or maybe a tad more. (I am sorry to say there are more obese people in Vegas than anywhere I have ever seen). The freshness and variety of the dishes on offer are as good as you can get. Best prime rib in town is at Lady Luck casino downtown, from $4.49, 4-11 pm. The Rio, behind Caesars Palace, a zippy and colourful place, vaunting the best looking cocktail waitresses, has the top steak 'n eggs breakfast ($2.99, 11 pm to 11 am). And if you have the energy, you can get a free 'funbook' from the Fiesta which contains (wait for it) $5.50 in gambling coupons, three two-for-one buffets, three free cocktails, a free appetizer and margarita, and a free ice cream.

Did I explain just why all these places are so generous to visitors?

They want you to stay on the property and gamble, that's why. What a sweet deal! *Las Vegas Advisor* is available from 3687, South Procyon, Las Vegas, Nevada 89103, credit cards (702) 252-0655, $5 per issue.

Bluffers

(37)
Bluff of the Year

The bluff of the week – no, more like the bluff of the year – occurred the other night in the big Omaha game at the Grosvenor Victoria casino.

Donnacha O'Dea, a popular figure on the international circuit, was dealt a good Omaha hand, 10-9-8-6. In Omaha a player must use two of his four cards in hand, with three from the flop, to make his final hand. Donn opened for £100.

The player on the button, one of the sharpest tournament players in the country, raised £300, which was a fairly reliable sign of aces. Donn called, five players in the pot.

The flop showed three spades: J-2-7.

No one bet. This, by the way, is Europe's biggest regular game. It is played in a friendly, even jocular, spirit, but can be very trappy. Low flushes are dangerous. Don had nothing. The turn card was another 7. Again everyone checked. It looked as if no one had a third 7 either. Now on the river another 7 came down, making trips on board!

J♠ 2♠ 7♠ 7♥ 7♦.

Anyone with a pair in hand now had a full house. The two players ahead of Donn checked. Obviously he could not bet with absolutely nothing. The fourth player, who was renowned as an aggressive competitor, also checked. But the last player to speak, who had raised on the opening round, came in with a bet of £800. He actually had £1,300 in front of him.

Fold, fold, and Donn saw his chance. He *check-raised*, betting through the strong player on his left, who could not call now, even if he had a pair. The man who had bet £800 reckoned Don must be sandbagging with the fourth 7, and saw no reason to toss in his last £500. He folded!

His mistake was making a moderate final bet instead of betting his whole stack, which Donn could not possibly have called. The pot was worth £3,900. At that price almost any final call is justified, even on a single ace (some thought) which is a bit far-fetched, even though it would have won. Not surprisingly after this coup, the losing player cracked up for a week.

Failed Bluff

One of the qualities which differentiate a good player from a great player is the ability to give up a bluff when it goes wrong. Here is a case where one player failed the test.

In a low level game of seven card stud, he was the opener showing A♣ with 9♥ 10♠ in the hole, and brought it in for £1 which was routine. There were three callers showing nothing much. On fourth street he caught the K♥ and decided to bet the hand as if he had something, £10. Two of the players immediately dropped.

The one player remaining, who played loosely but without much judgement, showed Q-8. Next card gave him a second 8, which he checked. The first bettor tossed in £20, to see what his opponent would do. Trip 8s would certainly justify a re-raise. The man merely called. On sixth street the first player caught one of his opponent's 8s, a heart, which was a useful defensive card, giving him a four flush plus an inside straight draw.

A: (9♥ 10♠) A♣ K♥ 6♥ 8♥
B: (? ?) Q♠ 8♣ 8♦ 3♣

Player A read his opponent for queens up, reckoning the man read him for a pair of aces trying to make two pairs. So he bet £50. B called, a shade reluctantly. Now the final card was dealt face down in the hole. B took a peek, counted out a pile of chips, threatening to bet big, then pulled his hand back and checked. This is normally a sign of weakness, trying to dissuade an opponent from betting. So A, who had failed to improve, decided to continue his bluff. He bet the rest of his money £75.

B havered and hesitated. This was not 'moody'. Although A's door card (first up-card) was off-suit, which was a pointer against his starting out to make a heart flush, he knew that A was a rock with a reputation always to have the absolute nuts when he bet. With a heavy sigh, B finally stuck his money in. A threw his hand in the discards. B had three 8s.

Another player across the table said jokingly to A: "So it's not true you never bluff!" A said: "I only wish I didn't!" I know, because A was me.

(39)
Tricky Dicky

He was a very successful poker player, and left the navy with several thousand dollars in winnings," noted the obituary of Richard Nixon in yesterday's *Independent*. This episode in Nixon's early life is worth recalling, because his winnings helped finance his first election campaign and set him on a political careeer.

Nixon was a disciplined player, rather over-tight and money-oriented. But in the kind of free and easy games that he played during his naval service on island bases out in the Pacific, that was a winning formula.

One of Nixon's fellow officers has recalled that one day he noticed Nick (as he was then known) lost in his thoughts. Finally Nick revealed what was bothering him: "Is there any sure way to win at poker?" he inquired.

His friend told him he didn't know of a sure way to win: but his own theory for draw poker was that you should never stay in unless you knew that you had everyone beaten at the time of the draw. Good advice! Anyway, Nick liked what he heard, and spent three or four days practising various plays, without money. Soon he became adept. "He never raised unless he was convinced he had the best hand."

In the next two months, Nick won $6,000 – a huge sum back in 1943.

Another friend from those days went so far as to declare: "Nick was as good a poker player, if not better than, anyone we had ever seen. He played a quiet game but he wasn't afraid of taking chances." Later on, from the eminence of the vice-presidency, Nixon deprecated his talent for poker and was distinctly coy about his winnings.

He applied very clearly, however, the principles of poker in his diplomacy. He took the view that if you didn't win the little pots, on minor matters – in dealing with China or the Russians – then you couldn't win the big pots, when issues of national importance came up. Nixon saw a like-minded leader in Moscow. "There is no doubt but that Khruschev would have made a superb poker player," Nixon wrote in 1962, at the time of the Cuban missile crisis. But of course Khruschev over-bet his hand.

Nixon was to make a similar kind of mistake over Watergate. The whole Watergate cover-up can be seen as a gigantic bluff, based on the calculation that Congress would never be able to call. That turned out to be a colossal misjudgement, because all the 'cards', in the form of conversations with his White House aides about the Watergate cover-up, were recorded on tape. When the hand was shown face up, the bluff was exposed.

Young Nick would surely have remembered that even though you may start with the best hand, you can still be outdrawn.

(40)

Two bluffers

It is always sensible to hold on to your cards, until the hand is over. What appears to be a certain loser can sometimes turn out a winner.

A case in point occurred the other night when two players were both bluffing, and each thought the other must have won the pot. It happened in a typical Hold 'em hand. The flop showed two diamonds.

3♦ 5♦ 10♣

Player A, who was an amateur from out of town, bet moderately and player B, who was a seasoned pro, raised the size of the pot. He only had two small diamonds in the hole, but this is a standard play at Hold 'em.

By raising strongly, he hoped to win the pot then and there, representing a big hand, such as ace-ten in the hole, or even low trips. If his opponent calls the bet, because he has, in fact, got something, the raiser still has two chances to hit his flush (which of course the other man will never suspect) if another diamond should fall on the fourth or fifth up-cards.

But Player A did not meekly call, he re-raised. Now player B is in trouble. His little ploy has run into a good hand but he has to call on the odds. All the money was now in the pot, some £200 from each man.

Fourth and fifth up-cards showed no improvement, so now it was a straightforward showdown. Each player waited for the other to show his hole cards.

Player A, who had the duty to show first, as the man whose last bet was called, gave a shame-faced grin and said, "I was bluffing!" and threw his cards to one side. Player B, the pro, who still held his hand, paused, and then as everyone waited expectantly, showed 2d and 6d – he had also been bluffing. Luckily for Player A, the cards he had thrown away had not not touched the 'muck' or pile of discards. If they had they done so, the rule is the hand is dead.

Bluffer's Excuse

The last card in seven card stud is the moment of truth. Players who have stayed in all the way have either got a hand already or, just as likely, are drawing to make their hand. How you decide what to do is a function of the way the hand has been bet, and how much money is involved.

The last point is crucial. If you are in the showdown with very few chips, there is nothing to think about. But suppose you and one oppponent both have a lot of chips left. Do you want to hit your hand? Drawing to a four flush against a possible two pairs, you may have to commit yourself all the way, and go much further than you wanted. In those circumstances, it is better to fold on sixth street.

If on the other hand you are drawing to two pairs, and there is a lot of money involved, you can check and let your opponent take the risk of betting.

Here is a case in point. I had got involved on an indifferent hand **(Q♠-7♦) Q♥** followed by **10♥ 3♣**. Another queen had dropped, so there was not much chance of improving. What persuaded me to go ahead was that I was up against Jock, a gambling kind of player who came in on **8♦-10♦-K♣**. I thought the king might have paired him but bet £25 anyway, to test the water. He called. With kings-up he would certainly have raised. My next card was a jack, no help, and he caught a 4. Now I bet £50 and after a moment's hesitation he called. We both had about £100 left.

D: (Q♠-7♦) Q♥ 10♥ 3♣ J♠
J: (x x) 8♦ 10♦ K♣ 4♠

I had to put him on a four flush, because he was on tilt. I watched him very closely as he took his last card, folded it into his down cards and slowly s-q-u-e-e-z-e-d them to take a look. He took a long, long time on this. Then he laid his cards down, leaned forward and paused a few seconds. I took all this as a sign of nerving himself to bluff the pot, because if he had hit his flush, he would have bet straight away.

He stuck in £100 and I called in a miscro-second, not giving myself time to have second houghts. "Do you have an ace flush?" he asked. "No, I don't," I told him, heart sinking. He turned over his hand as if to lay out a lower flush. But his last card was a heart, not a diamond.

"I misread my hand, Oh God, how could I do that!" he swore.

A bluffer's excuse if ever I heard one.

"We all do it," I assured him, raking in the pot.

Technicians

(42)

Poker Types

Forget the maths. Every poker game is defined by the personalities of the players. In a sense, they are always the same types, only the mix is diffferent. As a rough and ready guide, here are the five kinds of player to be found at any game, anywhere in the world.

1. Mr. Tight. This player sticks to the odds and plays like granite. He is easy to read but hard to win from. If he makes a bet, he is sure to have the goods. But in a free swinging, high-raising game he has no chance.

2. Johnny Gambler. Fast and furious, this player likes to bet it up at every opportunity. He has never heard of odds, and has no respect for opponents' cards. If he has any kind of a hand or an "out" he will go for it. On his day, a big winner – he needs to be, to make up for all the other losing nights.

3. Doc Doolittle. The Doc has been around a long time and knows a lot about poker. He is not afraid to run a bluff on a pair of deuces, but makes sure he keeps out of trouble on the big hands. A break even player or small winner.

4. Jack O'Toole. Plays for fun and conversation, always telling stories and holding up the game, quick to explain where you went wrong or why he was unlucky. Genial, fond of a quick one at the bar between deals, shrewd on occasion.

5. Jimmy Cleverclogs. A rustler in a sports shirt, Jim is quick, aggressive and hard betting. Knows the odds, but mixes up his game to make his play unread-

able. Occasionally goes overboard but is back next night, or next week, without a backward glance.

It is far more important at poker to know your man (or woman) than to rely on maths. The odds are merely a framework for play, like the lines on a tennis court. The character sketches above are, of course, a parody. In practice, good players change their style, like changing gears, according to the mood and pace of the game. The challenge of poker is to read your opponents: every hand that is played reveals something about each player's individual style – and also your own.

As a fast, action game, in which a series of rapid decisions is up to the individual (no partner, no team) involved, poker offers a stimulating outlet to the blandness and routine of suburban living hemmed in by jobs, mortgages and social responsibilities. It celebrates the Western virtues of the game's origins: true grit, daring and courage. Luck comes into it, but the luck evens out in the long run.

(43)

Hourly Rate

True pros at poker don't brood on the question "Did you win, did you lose?" They care, of course. But they think in a different way, not in terms of money won or money lost, but of their *hourly rate* in the game. This concept is based on what is known as positive expectation. In his clever book *The Theory of Poker*, now published in a new edition, David Sklansky explains the idea.

Forget, to start with, any idea of poker as "fun". That is not the point. The point for a pro is to maximize his positive expectation.

Suppose you have a full house in five card draw, Sklansky says. A player ahead of you bets. You know that if you raise the player will call. So raising appears to be the best play. However, when you raise, two players behind you will surely fold.

On the other hand, if you merely call the first bettor, you can be fairly confident that the two players behind you will also call. By raising you gain one unit, but by only calling you gain two. That is the higher positive expectation and the better play.

By making plays which always maximize positive expectation, the pro player hones his edge. It is a matter of skill, of judgement, of playing his cards better, winning more with good hands, losing less with bad hands. His positive expectation determines the return on the professional player's time, namely his hourly rate. This, rather than winning spectacular hands, is the bottom line.

For instance, if in draw lowball you see three players calling a £10 opening bet and then drawing two cards, which is a very bad play, you can say that every time they put in £10 they are losing an average of about £2. If they are doing this eight times an hour, it means these three players will lose about £48. You are one of four players who are approximately equal. This would give you, though you can never be as precise as this, about £12 an hour each. "Once you have decided what your hourly rate is," Skansky adds, "you should realize that what you are doing is earning. You are no longer gambling in the traditional sense."

(44)

Money Management

The term 'money management' is derided by the experts. Mason Malmuth, who is the most acerbic among gambling writers, declared in *Gambling Theory and Other Topics*: "I hate money management. I hate it because it is a bunch of junk." Mathematics Professor Peter Griffin, author of the classic *The Theory of Blackjack* (1979), dismisses the term as meaningless. Arnold Snyder, 'the Bishop', who is currently the most active writer and thinker on blackjack, explains that the reason all the experts say the idea is worthless is because so many hucksters try to con the public, by selling systems as a sure thing.

What is money management? It is simply a way of handling your bankroll. If, for example, you have £100 gambling money, you can stick it all on one number at roulette and have a huge win if the number comes up. If your number does not come up, at least you save a lot of time. At the other end of the scale, you can have a hundred £1 bets, and pass two or three agreable hours in the process. The odds of your winning on each individual bet do not change.

So is money management really a matter of how you organize your time? Yes and No. If you have a plane to catch, and want to have a final pull on a slot machine as you leave the casino, fair enough. But most people, obviously, want the gambling *experience* – they want to make their money last.

If you are in Las Vegas for three days with say, three

thousand bucks to gamble, it makes sense to divide the money into three portions, so you can play a thousand a day, and probably divide each thousand again into three, so you can afford, say, a mid-morning, a pre-dinner and a late-night spin, acording to taste.

The positive side of money management is that if you give yourself enough time, whatever game you play, you can expect to have a lucky streak or two, in between your losing runs. In gambling you want to give yourself the chance of hitting that streak.

In the long run, whether you play dice, punto banco, roulette or casino stud, the player will lose. The casino hold on roulette is around 20%, thanks to the accumulation of players' bets, even though each individual bet on a number is 'only' 2.7% against the player and 1.35% on red or black. But in the short run, you can get lucky. Money management, therefore, is a useful way of disciplining yourself so as to get the biggest bang for your buck.

(45)

Book Tokens

Now is the season of good will, also of book tokens. Here are half a dozen books on poker which would make excellent presents – if not to a friend then to educate yourself.

1. *Hold 'em Poker* by David Sklansky $17.50. The first and basic guide to Hold 'em, which is a must read, for the simple reason that everyone else has read it and plays by Sklansky's guidelines.

2. *Super System* by Doyle Brunson, $50. This is a high-powered guide to the main variations of poker, by world champion Brunson and friends, full of tremendous insights, albeit geared to the American rather than the British game.

3. *Poker Essays* by Mason Malmuth, $24.95. Erudite and perceptive analysis of casino poker, reprinted from *Card Player,* followed by an equally strong volume II.

4. *The Education of a Poker Player* by Herbert O. Yardley, $9.95.

This racy account of the author's derring-do in card saloons of the old West, mixed up with poker stories and modern espionage, has become a classic. My favorite quote: "There's something seductive about the smell of horses, moonlight, and wet dew glistening on the green grass... Separately, they're not compelling. As a whole, no girl can withstand them." The English edition has a neat foreword by Al Alvarez, in which he confesses he learned more about life from this little book than from reading Shakespeare, Eliot or Lawrence.

5. Alvarez in his own write is the author of *The Biggest Game in Town*, $3.95, an entertaining and revealing insight into the mentality of the top-flight Vegas professionals.

6. *Keno Runner* by David Kranes, $17.95. This weird, surreal but virtually unkown novel is my all-time favourite book about the experience of Las Vegas. The author, a university teacher, has a mystical feel for gambling. "Las Vegas isn't America ," is its theme, "America is Las Vegas."

Although you can't, as they say, learn poker from books, you can at least skim a few lessons on the plane getting there. All these titles are available from the Gambler's Book Club in Las Vegas, fax (702) 832 7594. Numbers 4 & 5 are published here by Oldcastle Books and Fontana.

(46)

Hot Flashes

Some players hit "hot flashes". The term describes loose aggressive players who come to a card room and manage to "run good" for six months or a year or maybe longer. They may never realize that players like themselves show up all the time. Such stars are very vocal about their success and critical of players who are content simply to "grind it out". But sooner or later they all go broke. "Being flashy and flamboyant doesn't get the chips," affirms poker author Mason Malmuth. "You need to play well."

Malmuth has now published a second collection, *Poker Essays, Volume II*, extending his reflections as a hard-playing, hard-thinking pro based in Las Vegas. These two books represent the most solid achievement of any writing on the modern game. Malmuth is first and last a technician, unashamedly so. What you might think of as the spirit or soul or essence of poker, the fun of the game, is absent from this work. What concerns the author is taking down the money.

Here is an example of his acuity, discussing Omaha high low eight-or-better. Is A♦ A♣ 10♥ 8♠ a better starting hand than K♦ K♣ 10♥ 8♠? You might take it for granted that a starting hand with two aces is far better than one with two kings. Malmuth questions this obvious assumption.

He ran a computer simulation over 25,000 hands: the first hand had a win rate of 11.37% against seven opponents who played random cards to the end, as against 11.88% for the second hand – which is not statistically significant. But the two kings hand had 2,069 'scoops' (wins of the whole pot because no low hand of 8 or better is made), as opposed to 1,581 scoops for the aces. This difference of 488 scoops is significant, he notes, not merely statistically but from the profit point of view. Scooping a pot is more than twice as profitable as splitting it.

Likewise, one might say, his two books are twice as valuable as the one. *Poker Essays* and *Poker Essays Volume II* by Mason Malmuth, Two Plus Two Publishing, 226, Garfield Drive, Henderson, Nevada 89014, price $24.95 each, plus postage $10.

5 Card Stud

(47)

Mr. Boyd Gets it Back

Bill Boyd, who came from a poor family in Arkansas some 80 years ago, was reckoned in his day to be the best five card stud player in America. "I'd rather catch frost on my winter peaches than play stud with Bill Boyd," was Amarillo Slim's tribute. Bill still sits down with the hard cases at Binion's Horseshoe in Las Vegas.

Five card stud is a strong and simple bluffing game, one card in the hole and one face up, followed by three more cards with a bet after each:

(x) x bet, x bet, x bet, x bet.

Here is one of Bill Boyd's coups. He had been beaten out of $50,000 by a boastful player who made a lucky out-draw, and who then left the big game to brag about his prowess at a lower level. One night Bill followed him down and the following hand developed.

Player: **(x) Q-4-4-10**
Bill: **(x) 9-3-3-Q**

At the opening, the queen bet $70 and Bill raised $200 on his 9. The other players passed. On the third card Mr. Show-off was quite sure he had best hand, whether Bill had paired his 9s or had an ace in the hole, and bet $500. Bill made it $1,000. His opponent merely called. (Of course he should have raised the roof, to win the pot then and there).

On the fourth card Show-off, feeling confident, bet $2,000. Bill called and raised $6,000. Naturally the man had to see. And on the last card Bill bet the pot, $18,600. The man called for what he had left, $16,100.

You guessed it – Bill had a 3 in the hole. His opponent who had queens wired simply could not believe Bill would have started out on a (3) 9. The pot was worth $50,800. Bill tipped the dealer $800 and said: "That makes me evens."

(48)

Johnny Moss

It was probably the most famous poker duel ever played, Johnny Moss v. Nick 'the Greek' Dandalos, in Vegas back in 1949. The game was five card stud. Benny Binion, the rapscallion gambler who founded the Horseshoe casino in Fremont Street, staged the game, as a way of attracting customers. They stood six-deep around the table. Other players came and went if they could put up a minimum of $10,000. Legend has it the game ran for five months.

Johnny was the best there was. Jimmy was a gambler seeking action. One particular hand everyone remembers. Moss was dealt **(9) 6** and bet $200 against the Greek's **8** showing. He raised it back $1,500. Next card for Moss was a **9** giving him a concealed pair. The Greek caught a **6**. Moss now bet $5,000 and the Greek came right back with $25,000. Moss just called. He was aiming to take down all the money on this one.

Fourth card Moss got a deuce and the Greek a trey. He checked to trap him and the Greek bet out, just as Moss wanted. So now Moss raised him back, high. The Greek called. There was $100,000 in the pot. Last card for Moss was a 3, the Greek caught a jack.

Nick the Greek: **(?) 8 6 3 J**
Johnny Moss: **(9) 6 9 2 3**

The Greek was high on the jack and bet $50,000. There was no way he could have paid so much in the hand to outdraw him, as Moss figured it. So he stuck all his money in. If the Greek called it would mean a half a million pot. He stayed quiet, as if pondering, and then observed: "Mr. Moss, I think I have a jack in the hole."

"Greek," said Moss, "if you've got a jack down there, you're liable to win yourself one helluva pot."

He had the jack. But that was okay with Moss. He knew that if his opponent was going to go on "chasing dreams", he would break him in the end. As indeed he did. Johnny Moss, three times world champion, a legend at the table, died in December, 1995, aged 88. He played in the World Series every year and usually wound up in the money. Vegas won't be the same without him.

(49)
The Kid

You cannot learn to play poker from books, but you can certainly get a lot of pleasure from books about poker. The most celebrated novel, now reissued, is *The Cincinatti Kid* by Richard Jessup. Many people who have never played poker will have seen the film, with Edward G. Robinson as Lancey 'The Man' and Steve McQueen as 'The Kid' who tries to beat him.

It is a short book but great fun. The game, you may recall, is five card stud, which has more or less dropped out of the poker repertoire to be overtaken by Texas Hold 'em. The key hand is a classic. The Kid has a queen of hearts in the hole and catches two tens on his second and third cards. Lancey shows seven and eight of hearts.

The Kid bets $500, thinking to take the pot without more ado, but to his surprise Lancey raises $300. (This is not really a credible bet, but let that pass). $1,850 in the pot, and the Kid, correctly, re-raises $2,000. Lancey calls. Fourth card is dramatic.

The Kid: (Qh) 10s 10d Qc
Lancey: (?) 7h 8h 10h

Nice one. The ten hearts is a ten the Kid cannot get, and he has a heart in the hole, which Lancey cannot catch. The Kid's two pairs, even without improvement, make him a huge favourite. But here he makes a curious mistake. He bets just $1,000, because he wants

Lancey in. But at that price, $1,000 to win a pot worth nearly $7,500, the call is irresistible.

What the Kid should have done is bet the size of the pot and make Lancey pay for the privilege. Instead, last card gives Lancey the 9h. The Kid catches another queen for his full house.

Here the Kid makes his second misjudgement. He bets the rest of his money – $1,420. What for? Lancey is certainly not going to pay to see him, unless by some miracle he has hit a straight flush. When Lancey raises him back $4,100 the Kid makes his worst mistake – he calls. And of course 'The Man' turns over the Jh in the hole. As he remarks in the immortal line: 'All you pay is the looking price. Lessons are extra.'

The Cincinatti Kid, No Exit Press, £4.99

(50)

Mr. Boyd

I had a Las Vegas coffee mug, with a royal straight flush pattern, which I was very fond of. I used it nearly every day for ten years. It was a little gift from Bill Boyd, reputed to be the best five card stud player there ever was. When I got home recently, the mug was broken. And next day I heard that Bill Boyd had died, at the age of 91, no doubt to join the great celestial poker game in the sky.

Bill Boyd, known to everyone as Mr. Boyd as a mark of respect, was special. He had grown up in Arkansas at the start of the century, drifted into poker, and discovered his talent. He ran the poker at the Golden Nugget in Vegas for 36 years until his retirement in 1982. He made a tremendous sucess of this venture, by establishing sensible rules and ensuring fair play. The poker room became the home of the game and the arbiter of standards, as Binion's Horseshoe is today.

When Texas Hold 'em became popular, a generation ago, five card stud died out as too mechanical. This was hard luck on Bill. He never mastered Hold 'em in the same way.

I only once saw Bill playing five card stud, but it gave me an idea of his style. He was playing heads-up against a fresh-faced man in a suit and tie. Bill was showing (?) 8-6-3-10 and his opponent (?) 8-7-3-10.

There was a lot of money on the table. The man checked and Bill made a pot-sized bet at him. As the man havered, Bill started a sort of sing-song in his twanging Arkansan accent: "Ya got a pair of 10s down there? Ya better raise it right now. Maybe you ain't got 10s. Ya got 8s, hunh? That'd be good, 8s back-to-back. Hey, we cain't both have 8s can we? Or didja catch 7s? Ya think that's good 'nuf, go ahead..." and so on.

The man sat there, like a rabbit in the headlights, staring at the cards. Finally he seized his chips, threatening to call. Then he stood up, grabbed his chips and fled, leaving the 70-year-old Bill sitting on his own.

It was against etiquette for me to ask Bill what his hole card was, but he told me anyway. "Pair of 6s."

"Weren't you taking a big risk?"

"He had ace in the hole, wouldn't have played it else."

Hold 'em

(51)

Hold 'em Basics

Texas Hold 'em is the most popular game in modern poker. It's a simple game – marked by fast action, strong betting and subtle card reading. As the name implies, the game came out of Texas and the South-West, where men are men, and not afraid to gamble. The name Hold 'em perhaps derives from players yelling 'Hold 'em!' at the dealer, to stop a card coming out which may break their hand. It requires judgement and courage in about equal measure to play well, and is the game of the World Championship in Las Vegas.

At Hold 'em players receive two cards in the hole, followed by five cards dealt out in common. The first three dealt together are called "the flop," a fourth card (known as "the turn") and a fifth card ("the river" as in down the river) follow. There is a betting interval at each stage.

(x x) bet x x x bet x bet x bet

Players may use either or both their hole cards with the cards in common to make their hand. The intricacy of the game comes from the positional factor. It makes a huge difference if you are next to the dealer and first to act, or sitting half way round the table, or last to act (10 can play). In early position, a player needs high cards to open (pairs or ace-x or two high suited or straight cards), because of the risk of being raised round the table. But as the initiative moves around, players must decide if the pot justifies raising, or opening on lesser holdings. In last position, if there are no raises to come, a player might find it worth playing on almost anything, even 7-2 off-suit, the worst hand at Hold 'em (because it cannot improve on the flop to either a straight or a flush). Who knows – the flop might come up 7-7-2.

The cards in common mean that play is often very finely shaded. eg. Who wins the following hand?

A: A♣ J♥
Flop: A♠ Q♦ 9♦ 4♠ 9♠
B: A♦ 8♦

Answer: it's a split pot, two pairs aces and 9s with a queen. A's jack of hearts is irrelevant.

Hold 'em is best played pot limit. American casinos mostly play limit raise games, say $10 before the flop and $20 after it. This makes the game a lot less dangerous (the casinos want the players to survive, so the house can cut each pot played) but still requires good judgement. British casinos (which make a session charge) usually play pot limit. If you want action, that is where it is.

Going on Tilt

Going on tilt, like most other aspects of human behaviour, has been studied by psychologists. The two most common tilt-inducing situations are 'bad beats' and 'needling.' In the former case, for example, you might lose a hand holding trip aces to a man who started out with 2-4 and catches a low straight. This is, in fact, only one of those freaks of probability that are always cropping up, but it hurts. Needling is when someone chooses to make a personal comment, such as telling you that you misplayed the hand anyway.

Going on tilt happens when such an experience (common enough) induces a desperate desire to get even, by chasing the betting. The result is a loss of control, evidenced by hurtling more and more of your money away, in a bid to recoup more and more losses. After it's over, you hate yourself for it. Everyone else round the table, of course, loves it. This is what going on tilt means, manifested in its most self-destructive form by moving up to higher stakes.

One way of preventing going on tilt is to leave the table. Players can always pick up early warning signals when things are going wrong. The other way is to work on your emotions, as in a mental gym, to regain control. It is not a matter of suppressing the emotion. The point is to make the effort to work on it, the aim being to return to one's normal mode of play as quickly as possible. The consistent winner may go on tilt for a couple of hands or so. The consistent loser, say the psychologists, will remain on tilt for hours, days, or even months.

Here's an example of going on tilt, which (hard to believe) I went through myself. It was high stakes Hold 'em. I had been losing and winning back a little bit, and losing all night, and then went through a two-hour lean spell, as can happen, when no good cards came to hand. Finally I got down to my reserve pile of chips, and vowed that if that last ditch was breached, it was time for bed. Out, over, *finito*.

Comes a hand when everyone calls a hefty raise before the flop. I had 10-9 suited. Of course I called. And the flop comes 9-5-3. At last!

Everyone checked around to me and I let 'em have it. Whereupon some diabolical fellow at the other end of the table check-raised me. I know he has me beat, I know he must have trips 5s or 3s. But at that point a sort of blood haze of frustration occludes sensible judgement. So in it all goes, to the last chip. Thank you, and good night.

(53)

Do You or Don't You?

A typical Hold 'em hand poses the question: do you or don't you? Do you go all in or do you drop. Although calling is also an option, it is not usually justified in heads-up confrontations. Here is a case in point, between Sean, a gambling sort of player, and Gus, an old salt.

Sean raised, as he likes to do on speculative hands, and Gus called on 9♦-J♦. Everyone else dropped. The flop showed a straight and a flush draw.

S: (? ?)
Flop 8♦ 10♦ 2♣
G: (9♦-J♦)

Sean, first to speak, bet and Gus called. The turn (fourth card) produced a 6♥. Now Sean bet the pot. How should Gus react? It's no use calling along. He has to find out there and then if Sean really has anything or is trying it on. So Gus raised back £45. He got his answer immediately. Sean re-raised £180. Gus now knew virtually for certain that he was up against a low straight. Should he fold?

The way you work out these calculations is as follows: Gus has a total of 15 cards which can win for him. Nine diamonds to make a flush (the assumption is that Sean has not got diamonds) and six cards to make a higher straight (three queens outside the diamond suit and three 7s, (leaving out of account Sean's unseen cards in the hole). There are 46 cards which Gus has not seen. The chances of Gus *not* making it on the river (last flop card) are therefore 31 (46 minus 15) divided by 46= 0.67. He is, therefore a 2-1 underdog to win the hand, and the pot is offering him precisely 2-1 for his money. Call!

Poker players do not make such fine calculations at the game. Every competent player knows the rule of thumb that pot odds must match, or preferably exceed, the odds of catching the cards to make a winning hand. In addition to which, there are *implied* odds: Sean had a further 90 chips left, which he would certainly toss in if Gus bet (giving him 2.5 to 1 for his money). In this example, Sean had 7-9 off-suit in the hole. Gus lost, but he did have the dour satisfaction of having made the right play.

(54)

A Fiver Saved

S tewart Reuben, who has a reputation as one of the sharpest players around town, made a witty play the other night. In a £2,000 pot, he declined to call the showdown for a mere fiver.

The game was 'Irish', which is a souped-up version of Texas Hold 'em, much favoured by players for its fast action. At Irish Hold 'em, instead of two cards dealt in the hole, as in the regular game, players receive three, four or even five cards, which means they can make far better starting hands. After 'the flop', or first three up cards dealt in common, the players then discard their additional hole cards, keeping just two in the hand, as usual. (The Irish player Colette Docherty told me that 'Irish' was named after a bright idea by her son Peter.)

Anyway, Stewart was dealt a pair of queens and three 'rags' in the hole and found **Q-J-10** on the flop. Only one other player bet. Naturally, Stewart threw threw the three low cards and kept the queens. The next card off was an ace.

(Q Q) Q J 10 A

Now, if this opponent has a king in the hole (probably with an ace), which is more or less certain when he bets, Stewart is beaten. But he has nine 'outs', cards which can win for him. He can improve to a full house (there are three jacks, three tens, and two aces left in the deck, any one of which may fall on the fifth up card; and of course the case queen for four of a kind); plus three chances of catching a king, which would make him a high straight to share the pot. So when his opponent bet £500 into a £1,000 pot, Stewart called him.

A further point in his calculations was that the other player has read him for a straight, too. So if a pair did happen to flop on the last up-card, Stewart would almost certainly get called when he bet, winning a really big pot. But the final up-card was no help, a six. At which point the man tossed in a £5 chip – equivalent to saying, "All right, we've both got a high straight, let's split the pot."

At which point, Stewart looked at the fiver – and folded! There was much amazement round the table. Why fold for a measly fiver, when the pot was worth £2,000? Surely there was 'value' in calling, at odds of 400 to 1. Stewart took a different view: "A fiver is a fiver. I knew I was beaten. What's the point in throwing it away? It would be like being offered 400 to 1 that 1 + 1 = 4."

55

Big Slick

S ome poker hands are notoriously tricky to play, none more so than 'Big Slick', as Ace-King at Hold 'em is known. An example analysed by poker writer Mason Malmuth comes from a $6-$12 limit raise game. It shows the kind of reasoning involved in Hold 'em.

The player concerned was a lady, a fairly solid player, still learning. Two seats off the button, she raised with **A♠ K♣**, after a weak player had limped in from middle position. The player on the button (last to speak) re-raised, the small blind called, the limper called, and the lady called. The implication was that the player on the button had a very strong hand.

The flop was **K♥-K♠-J♣** which looked perfect for her. It was checked round to her and she decided to check along. In this situation it was almost automatic for the button to bet: she could then check-raise him and catch one or both of the other players in the pot as well. But the button checked!

It certainly seems wrong to give the other players a free card. So what could he have? Most likely A-K as well, possibly a pair of aces. (His idea was to get a double bet on the turn.) The turn card was **6♦**. The player who had originally limped in now bet out (trip 6s?) and everyone called. The river card was the **A♦**.

(A♠ K♣) K♥ K♠ J♣ 6♦ A♦

The small blind checked, the limper checked, the

young lady bet and the player on the button raised. Now we know what he's got! It had to be A-K or aces wired. The others dropped and the lady *re-raised*. Did she make the right play? asks Malmuth. If she had put the opponent on A-K or A-A, she was either tied or beaten. Ergo, there was no equity in re-raising. The button merely called – apparently he was afraid of four kings – and showed his pocket rockets.

What was the lady's major error? She made the classic mistake of just playing the strength of her own hand, without considering what her opponent held. And she failed to read hands through all playing rounds.

56

Pump it or Dump it

Here's another example showing why Hold 'em is the game where you 'pump it or dump it', that is, raise or fold rather than just call along.

Stewart Reuben, playing in Las Vegas, found A♥-K♦ in the hole and raised before the flop. Several players called. The flop came down A♦ 10♥ 7♦. He bet the pot, $500. The next player raised $1,500, which left him $4,500 remaining. Everybody folded round to Stewart.

Poker is not a science, but with so many people in the pot, no one could have thought Stewart's bet was a bluff. Nor, in such a situation, could his opponent be on a steal.

S: (A♥-K♦) A♦ 10♥ 7♦

The tough customer Stewart was up against might reasonably hold A-A, 10-10, 7-7, A-10, J♦-10♦ or 9♦-8♦. All these hands were favourites to win against Stewart, but the last two were the most likely possibilities.

Stewart called, which is a clear exception to the general rule against being a 'calling station'. His reasoning was as follows: if a diamond, jack or 6 were to fall, he could always check and pass if the other man bet out; or if a diamond or a jack did fall, his opponent might decide to trap check. Then Stewart would have been in in the enviable position of drawing to the 'nuts' (another diamond or a queen.) Yet another possibility is that the diamond might come on fourth street and the opponent (holding a made hand rather than a drawing hand) might fear Stewart had made the nut flush (allowing him to bluff on the river). For all its aggressive style, Hold 'em is a very chessy game.

The next card was a blank. Now checking and calling would be feeble in the extreme. Stewart bet the $4,500. His opponent called. The last card was also a blank and Stewart had the satisfaction of raking in a $13,500 pot.

The only drawback was that no Vegas pro who saw or heard about the hand would in future take Stewart for a tourist, if they ever had to start with.

(57)

Star Chasing

"You shouldn't play this game at all!" protested the Middle East player, half-joking, half-seriously, admonishing an habitual loser. "You don't have any idea what it's all about!" The other man smiled sheepishly as he pulled up another hundred. He knew, presumably, the truth of the advice he was offered. But that was not, for him, the point. Playing cards was his way of enjoying himself – and why not?

The motive for playing poker does not lie, solely, in winning money.

True, that is how you 'keep score'. But there are one or two other attractions of the game, such as amusing company, the thrill of high stakes, the test of character (notably your own) under pressure, in a word, the challenge.

For me, one of the main attractions of poker is the extraordinary variety of players it brings in. There are no social barriers. So when the losing player left the table for a minute, I ventured to reproach the Middle Easterner for criticizing him. "He likes to play, that's all!" "You mean it is good for the rest of us to have a 'star' in the game?" "Would you say that he was so foolish," I countered, "if he chose to spend a couple of hundred quid on a night at the opera and dinner in a restaurant?"

As it happened, I liked the big loser for different reasons. He had a sense of humour, took his losses well and, when he got lucky, did not crow about winning. We are all of us 'stars' when we come up against stronger players. And once in a while, as in all sports, the lower-ranked player will sock it to a big winner.

In Las Vegas, for instance, it is a tremendous thrill playing against players of championship renown – somewhat akin to star-chasing. They, for their part, are deliberately 'playing down' and sometimes get caught. After all, if there were no losers at poker there would be no winners either. So if you do happen to feel guilty about taking money from someone who clearly hasn't a clue, better stifle your qualms and give him a book on poker. That won't do any good either, but it's the thought that counts.

(58)

Tight as a Tortoise

It is difficult to winkle out a very tight player, who folds almost every hand on principle. Here's an example of how I managed it the other night in a low limit Hold 'em game. The monetary gain was small but the satisfaction quotient very high.

Sitting on the big blind I found 2-4 off-suit. My opponent, who plays like a tortoise which never sticks its neck out, had opened in 6th position, indicating he had a hand, probably ace-x. The flop came down 4♣ 4♠ 2♦.

I checked my full house, obviously. But the tortoise, knowing that I play almost as tight as him, checked along. The turn card was a 7♠. I checked again and again he followed. The river card was a queen of spades, which meant a possible flush.

(2♥ 4♦) 4♠ 4♣ 2♦ 7♠ Q♠

This was my last opportunity to bet my hand, but I checked one final time, trying to look worried. This finally induced the tortoise to bet an heroic £5. I raised 5, representing a flush. And the tortoise, having poked his head out so far, had the temerity (knowing me, knowing you) to get his feet wet too. He re-raised with a bet of 25, taking me for a low flush. I socked it right back and he felt obliged to call me down. He didn't have ace-x of spades in the hole after all, but 2-2, giving him a lower full house than my 4s full.

A couple of other players at the table began ribbing

him. "How could you re-raise?" they smirked. "That was money down the drain!" The tortoise blinked, muttered something about calling for value, and retreated into his shell.

We had both been trying the same tactic. In fact, a tight image is a good, winning style for Hold 'em. If players think an opponent is so tight he will only play hands like aces and kings, they are inclined to fold when he raises, especially if there is an ace on the flop. If they do call, the tight player can put them on a hand. The tortoise would have done better to bet on the flop, and when I called, pull his head right back in.

(59)

Crazy Bill

I'll give you £1,000 if you can tell me how I could lose this hand!" a highly excitable loser, as players from the orient tend to be, protested the other night. "First to speak at Hold 'em, I open with two kings, it's raised before the flop, I re-raise, two players call. The flop comes K 9 4 off-suit. I bet the pot, £100. One man – this idiot – calls. Next card is a 5. I bet the pot again, £300. Last card is a queen. Of course I bet the size of the pot, £900. What can he have?"

(K K)
Flop: K♠ 9♥ 4♣ 5♦ Q♠
(? ?)

"And this idiot, this madman, this..." At this point the narrator, waving his cigarette around almost set fire to the cards, "this man, Crazy Bill, he raised me back! I have to call. I thought he misread his cards. Do you know what he played on? He played on J-10 to hit an inside straight. You explain that, I give you £1,000."

I could explain it, but I never the got the chance. My friend was too consumed by the passion of being hard done by to listen. Actually there are two explanations. The first is simply that the man who won the pot is an habitual loser. He is going to throw away a fortune on bad plays, in return for the occasional lucky break. The player on the losing end of such a freak draw should smile at fate, and be grateful that such an opponent will stay in the game, and many future games, when his luck will not hold.

The second explanation concerns odds. On the flop Crazy Bill has a draw to an inside straight 9-10-J-K. There are only four cards (the four queens) in the deck to make his hand. Subtracting the 5 cards he has seen (2 in his hand and 3 on the flop) from the deck, he has 4 chances out of 47 to hit his hand, near enough 11-1, and two cards to try it. On the money odds of only 2-1, this is terrible. But if he hits the elusive queen and the kings-in-the hole player has a lot of chips, so that Crazy Bill can raise him back, he stands to win a gigantic pot for his gamble, and wreak havoc round the table. So was he such a mug?

Answer: unless you are as reckless with money as Crazy Bill, don't try it. The calculation above overlooks the fact that he can hit his card and still lose. After the flop, if any running pair falls on board (eg. Q-Q or a Q plus a 9 or 4), the trip kings improve to a full house. If there were no bad players at poker games, there would be very few winners.

(60)

Incredible Hand

"**Y**ou'll never believe this hand!" Michael was so stunned he rang me down in the depths of rural France from the card room at the Grosvenor Victoria to tell me about it. It was £100 Hold 'em, a medium-sized game, the hundred pounds being the minimum amount of chips a player has to put up to play, with antes merely £1-1-2. Most people put up three or four hundred, sometimes a thousand. But this unknown Indian player suddenly appeared out of nowhere and plonked £10,000 worth of chips down in front of him.

First hand Michael found **A-9** off-suit in the hole, raised before the flop and got two callers. Down came **A-4-10**. The opener bet the pot, £150, the Indian and Michael both called.

Next card was a **4**, pairing the board: **A 10 4 4**.

Player A now bet £300. The Indian gentleman called, Michael decided his **9** kicker was not good enough, and folded. Last card was a **6**, no flush, no straight draw.

The first man now bet £600 at the pot. The Indian thought and thought and, finally, called. Player A smiled. "You win," he said, turning over a **7-2** off-suit – the worst possible starters at hold 'em. He had been trying some esoteric super-bluff. The Indian, however, turned over a **3-2** off-suit. He could not even beat the board. In fact his only hope, and that merely to split the pot, would be if the bettor had also held **3-2**.

A: (2♣-7♦) A♥-10♠-4♣ 4♦ 6♥
B: (2♦-3♠)

The point of this story is the extraordinary fact that the bluffer chose to *show* his (quite obviously losing) 7-2, rather than muck his cards in the deck. Ninety-nine people people out of a hundred would feel so embarrassed by exposing such a pathetic hand, they would prefer *not* to show their cards at all. But in the event the 7 took it!

Obviously the Indian visitor did not understand the game. Indeed in a home poker game he would probably be given his last bet back, because he called in a situation in which he could not win. So why did player A choose to show his ineffable 7-2? He wanted the newcomer to see how loosely he played.

Point taken.

61

Dream Hand 1

I t was the hand of the decade, a dream hand, perfectly played. It happened in a $5-$10 blind pot-limit game of Texas Hold 'em at the Mirage in Las Vegas. The player in the big blind found two black queens in the hole. When the action came round to him there were four players involved at $20 a player, all of whom had better than $5,000 on the table. He just flat called.

Out came the flop:

Q♥ Q♦ 9♦

So our hero **(Q♠ Q♣)** flopped quads. It's happened before. But look how he played them! First to speak, he made a quick $50 bet. He could be playing anything – a queen, a flush draw, straight draw, a nine paired. The player in seat 3, a rambunctious business type, called after much hesitation. His acting-up probably meant he already had a 9s full house **(9♠ 9♣)**. Player number 4 folded but seat 6 called. It looked as if he might be on a diamond flush draw. Now seat number 8 hesitated a long time and finally raised $200. He could have low diamonds or a high pair in the hole. Our man with quads in seat number 1 thinks and then just calls. Seats 3 and 6 also call.

The next flop card turns the ace of diamonds! Number 1 checks. It's obvious someone has hit a diamond flush. The key is that seats 3, 6 and 8 each believe the queens are split around the table. Number 8 now bets out $1,000. He must have made the nut flush (**K♦ x♦**). Seat number 1 calls immediately. Seat number 3 merely calls with his full house 9s. Seat 6 calls – he knows 8 has a higher flush but perhaps he is holding (**Jd 10d**) for a straight flush and can't resist it.

Comes the river card. It's the **9♥**, giving the actor-manager quad 9s!

Seat number l must be tempted to check again, but he is cleverer than that. He fires out $5,000. Reason: he doesn't want seat number 3 to check along hoping for a raise from one of the flushes or presumed queens fulls, which may not come. Now seat number 3 has given up his acting. As soon as 1's chips are in the pot he shoves forward his stack with glee. Of course seats 6 and 8 went fast. Seat number 1 made his all-in call and quietly laid down his four queens, without a blink.

The player in seat 3 clutched his chest. It wasn't the money but the embarrassment. He never had the best hand. Player number 1, who showed a rare command of the game and his opponents, read him all the way. Reporting this graphic encounter in the monthly magazine *Card Player*, Raymond 'Iceberg' Sitra asks: could you have played it better?

62

Dream Hand 2

"**I** won't sleep all night," moaned Ali, after yet another (it's his speciality) horrible outdraw at Hold 'em. Ali raised ace-queen of hearts in the hole and the flop came down queen of diamonds, 9-7 hearts. This is a Hold 'em player's dream hand. He has flopped the top pair with an ace kicker, in case an opponent also holds a queen; plus he has a flush draw to the 'nut', or top, flush to go with it. What could be better that that? Especially when some Japanese player who evidently doesn't know his sushsi from his elbow calls the bet (the pot had been well raised by Ali before the flop) for £40. Next card is 4 diamonds – no sweat. The Japanese player could hardly have stuck around with low cards in the hole. Ali bet £120 this time, the size of the pot. The Japanese gentleman blinked behind his specs and tentatively pushed his chips forward. He had a pile of about £800 in front of him. Last card was a real nothing, two of diamonds. So Ali stuck it all in – well, wouldn't you?

Ali (A♥ Q♥)
Q♦ 9♥ 7♥ 4♦ 2♦
J (? ?)

As the Japanese pushed his chips forward to call Ali's bet, he murmured, ever so politely, the word "Frush". He showed J-6 diamonds in the hole. What persuaded him to stay on such a hand, after the big bet on the flop, Heaven alone knows. Could he really have expected to catch two more diamonds on 4th and 5th street, to hit a 'back door' flush? The problem of trying to read poker players who don't know anything about the game is that normal judgements are inoperable.

Proof was provided a few hands later later, when the Japanese gentleman hit yet another miracle flush, and didn't even realize his good fortune. His opponent, an experienced player, turned over a pair of kings in the hole. The Japanese bowed slightly, smiled, and threw his cards away – showing, as he did so, a spade flush. Unfortunately for him, the rule is that once you muck your hand in the discards, the hand is void.

He showed no ill feeling, or any emotion whatever, at this reversal. So a few minutes later, I ventured to commiserate with him on such an unlucky turn, even though he had by now amassed about £1,500 worth of chips. "No ploblem," he replied. "Next hand I hit a stlaight frush."

(63)

Straight Flush Clash

"**H**aven't seen that happen in 30 years," claimed one of the dealers at London's Victoria casino. He might have exaggerated a touch, but this was certainly an exceptional hand. Darren returned from supper, having had a glass or two of red wine to loosen up, and picked up **J♦-10♦**. That is, potentially, a very powerful hand at Texas Hold 'em, so he raised the opening bet and got one caller, Sasha, a fairly strong gambler who was playing with plenty of chips.

> D: (J♦-10♦)
> S: (? ?)
> The flop came 7♦ 8♦ A♥

Darren, who is known as a solid player, bet the pot £200. Sasha called and raised £600. Darren was in a post-prandial mood but he wanted to play this hand to the limit anyway. He can hit 9d for a straight flush, which most players find an irresistible draw at Hold 'em, any diamond for a lesser flush, and of course an off-suit 9 to fill his inside straight. He wanted to get his money in then and there, because he reckoned that if a diamond happened to fall, his own hand was so obvious his opponent would not pay him off.

So he re-raised Sasha £1,800, who capped the sequence by re-reraising the rest of his money. (As you may have surmised, this was a big game, far beyond the ambitions of your poker correspondent.) The dealer stacked up a glorious pile of red and orange hundred and thousand pound chips in the centre, some £7,000.

With all the money in, everyone at the table held their breath. First card off was a black 5, which put Sasha ahead on a small pair. Then on the river came the elusive, will o' the wisp, card of Darren's heart's desire, the 42-1 shot 9♦. It was the card *both* players had wanted, because Sasha had 5♦-6♦ in the hole, for a straight flush too. His moment of triumph was over in an instant.

"Straight flush to the jack," announced the dealer, pointing to Darren's cards. Everyone gawped. These things do happen in books but seldom in real life.

"Why did you re-raise on the flop, when it looked like he had paired an ace, possibly the A♦?" I asked Darren next day. "I had 9 outs for the flush and three 9s for the straight, and two draws to hit," Darren explained. "So I thought I was favourite. Besides, he might not have an ace in the hole. After all, this is Hold 'em."

64

Straight Flush Loser

Here's a bizarre case where a player hit a straight flush, won the hand and lost £750 in the process. It happened at the Holland Casino's hugely successful poker festival last week. In the big no-limit Hold 'em tournament a special prize of 1% of the total money was offered for the best hand of the night.

Player A, on the small blind (first ante), found 2♠-4♠ in his hand. He called, as a small bet for value against the big blind (higher ante). The flop came 3♠-5♠-10♥. Just these two players involved, so A checked. Then on the next card K♠ fell, giving A his flush. Player B had about 3,000 chips left. Player A, first to speak, now bet 2,000. Player B, who presumably had a king in the hole, called. And the last up-card was 6♠, giving A an unexpected straight flush.

(2♠ 4♠) 3♠ 5♠ 10♥ K♠ 6♠

What should A do? Answer: not bet a cent! With four spades on board, player B is not going to call with his last thousand chips, unless he has a spade too. But in his excitement at hitting such a powerhouse, A bet the thousand. B folded of course. As the hand was not seen to the finish, it could not therefore qualify for the best hand prize. If Player A had simply checked, Player B would have checked along and the straight flush would have been seen. And, as it turned out, lifted the prize.

Unusually, the event was won by a young Dutch woman player Belinda Blokker, who often plays in London. She had her share of luck, as you need to do, especially at the final heads-up stage. With blinds up to 30,000 and 60,000 chips, this duel is always a bit of a shoot-out. Her opponent bet all-in. Belinda had already committed 60,000 as big blind, plus 6,000 ante. If she surrendered the hand, her opponent would be back to level pegging with her. She looked down at her cards. 3-7.

As she put it: "One side of my head said: 'I can't call!' The other side of my head said: 'I must call!'" So she called. I don't believe I could face exposing such a pitiful hand to the laughter of the spectators. But better players than I am assure me it was the correct play. Against two higher cards 10-8, Belinda was getting 3.5 for her money on a 2-1 shot. And what happened? A 3 and a 7 flopped.

65

The Right Card

Again and again I am struck by how catching one card just when you need it can make or break the whole game. Just like, I suppose, one accurate pass or one mis-kick can make or mar a whole football match. It fell the right way for me at Hold 'em the other night. Sitting on the button in an eight-handed game, I found A♣-J♣ in my hand.

Cheeky Chow, on my right, raised the opener £10 and I called. My hand is not good enough to re-raise, though in a tournament one might well blast it, to try and take the pot then and there. The opener, Jimmy Flim, who was a computer programmer by training but a fire-raiser by nature, called. Down came the flop

7♥-10♣-J♦

I thought my hand was good but to my surprise Chow bet the pot, £30. Given that he was a fairly steady player and had raised the opener, I put him on a high pair, aces or kings. I called instantly, because I did not want to give myself time to think about it and pass – my real aim was to trap Jim (who had out-played me on many previous occasions). This time he just called.

Now on the turn a 9♣ came down, making a possible straight on board. Jim bet £100 and sat staring straight ahead, as is his way. Chow looked at his hole card, sighed and havered. Finally he called, all-in. I was now almost certain he had a high pair in the pocket but

I wanted to catch Jim. I put him on a speculative inside straight draw, with something like a 7-6 in his hand. This was the way he liked to play against 'value' players like me.

So I stuck it right back to him with a re-raise, putting him all-in. After all, I had top pair with top kicker, a nut flush draw with a club and an inside straight draw if an 8 came down on the river. Jim called, as I knew he would. The last card, as luck would have it, was a low club. Chow had a pair of kings – he had called the previous bet in the hope of catching a queen for top straight. I had completely mis-read Jim who showed an 8 for a low straight.

As I raked in the pot I mumbled an apology. "No problem," said Jim, "these things happen". As indeed they do. But having won this big pot my confidence soared in inverse proportion to the others losing their nerve, and I smashed the game in short order. That is Hold 'em, but really it all came down to one lucky break.

66

End Game

Three players came down to a surprising finish in a tournament at the Victoria casino's recent summer festival of poker. It was 3.40 am., and under the rules of the tournament, if an event was still not decided by that time (the casino having to close at 4 am. anyway), just three more hands more would be dealt, and the prizes awarded on chip totals. Of course it would be far preferable to resume the final the next night, after the players had had a sleep, so as to fight it out to a clear finish. But this was the way the Vic arranged it, as all the players knew beforehand, on the grounds that some players might not be available the next day.

This event was no limit Hold 'em. Player A was leading with 80,000 chips, feeling pretty happy. Player B had 65,000 in chips. And player C, who was an experienced sports player from Philadelphia, one Myron Rosenbaum, was lying third on 60,000. How should play go, when the last three hands of the night were announced?

Myron knew the score. He had nothing to lose. However the final hands panned out, he was bound to finish no worse than third place. Even if he lost all his chips, that result was guaranteed. So the obvious play was to bet the lot, "all in". If he got lucky and beat either of his two opponents, he would finish in first place. Even if they did not play, he would nick second spot, just on the antes, which were running at 8,000 a hand. So on the penultimate hand Myron, player C first to speak, stuck all his chips in on a pathetic **Q-7** off-suit. Player A felt he was caught in a sandwich, not knowing if Player B was going to call behind him or fold.

Player B, however, sussed out immediately what was happening. He stood second but if he folded, his reduced chip total meant he would automatically be relegated to third place. So he called, on a fair hand as it happens **J-10**.

Player A, hanging on as chip leader at that point, evidently missed the significance of the last three hands being played out to determine the result. The right move was to play, whatever cards he held. In his situation, he can do no worse than finish second. Even if he got busted, he still has 15,000 more chips, over and above either of the other two players, which was enough to ensure him second spot. By not playing in the hand, he simply allowed one of the other two to overtake him, regardless.

As luck would have it, Myron caught a second queen on the flop, and zoomed up into first place. First prize was £14,550 as against £7,275 and £4,365 for second and third. Nice one Myron.

67

Hold 'em Excellence

Fashions come and go but Texas Hold 'em is currently the most popular of all poker games. It is so simple – two cards in the hole and five dealt face-up in common – that everyone thinks they can play it. But the game is almost infinitely subtle and deceptive. No wonder that books and manuals on how to play Hold 'em keep on coming out.

The latest is *Hold 'em Excellence*, sub-titled 'From beginner to winner', by Lou Krieger, a player-writer out on the West coast. Here's an example of subtlety in card reading, though it turned out badly for the author. He was last to act, holding pocket kings and re-raised a very strong player on his right. The flop came down:

A♣ K♥ 4♠

His opponent bet, Krieger raised, and got re-raised. Krieger knew his man so well he was sure he would not have bet if he'd flopped a set of aces (trips). He would merely check and re-raise on the turn (4th street). So he put him on A-K with a smaller possibility he held a hand like A♥-J♥. The turn card was the **6♥**. He bet and Krieger raised. His opponent called.

If he had flopped a set of aces he would have now re-raised, since this would have been the best possible hand. Now Krieger was almost certain the man held A-K. As his opponent knew Krieger equally well, he would not have called with less than two pairs. When the **8♥**

fell on the river (last card), he bet, Krieger raised and he re-raised.

Now the author knew his original assessment that his opponent held A-K was wrong. He had to have a hand like A♥-J♥ and had tried to steal the pot on the turn, with top pair and a reasonably good kicker.

Each player, by virtue of their bets, raises and re-raises, was defining his hand in terms of what he presumed the other was holding. "Although my analysis was correct," Kriger laments, "I was too late to save myself any money."

Hold 'em Excellence, B & F Enterprises, Inc., 2375 East Tropicana Avenue #281, Las Vegas, Nevada 89119, $30 including postage.

(68)

Monster Pot

"What goes around, comes around," they say in Las Vegas. In poker terms, this means: if you are patient enough luck will even out, the cards have a way of coming back, wrongs will be righted. Good advice, and never better illustrated than in a losing run which hit a friend of mine recently, journalist Don Larrimore.

Playing a game of $4-$8 limit Hold 'em down at Binion's Horseshoe, Don got beaten in a period of four hours fifteen minutes on the following succession of premium hands: A-A once, A-K suited twice, K-K six times, Q-Q twice and J-J once. An incredible run, as you will agree. Yet at the end of this period, he manged to come out $35 ahead.

The reason Don emerged unscathed lay in a remarkable hand, a Hold 'em player's dream, which was dealt as follows.

Don sitting last found 6-7 of spades in the hole. There was a pre-flop raise from seat six, which five players called, which at 6 x $8 boosted the pot to $48. Out came the flop: (see next page)

To his surprise, Don found he had a straight flush made. Normally, such a hand attracts little action, but this time it was different. Player A took the lead with his Ks-Qs, player B with 9-9 raised, player E with 5-5 came along for the ride, Player F with As-4s re-raised, Don meekly called, and the pot got jammed. This round was worth 5 x $32 = $160.

The turn card produce an 8, giving players B and E

	B	**C**	
A	9-9	x	**D**
Ks-Qs			x

Dealer	**Flop**	**E**
	5s-8s-9s-8-2	5-5

Don		**F**
6s-7s		As-4s
	H **G**	
	x Js-10s	

full houses, which they bet and raised like there was no
tomorrow. G with a straight flush draw had to call. This
round yielded 4 x 32 = $128. On the river, which pro-
duced an irrelevant deuce, Don finally permitted himself to take a raise. By now, everyone understood something weird was happening. But for $8 it would require
almost super-human restraint not to call, so the others
came along, adding another $64 to the pot.

The total pot which Don scooped was $400, which
is enormous for the $4-$8 game. He was still not quite
out of trouble on the session, but after that he was dealt
A-K suited and J-J, which both stood up. At that point,
he pushed his chair back and withdrew to the bar.

(69)

No Fold 'em Hold 'em

Fast and loose, the Los Angeles card clubs are like a new gold rush of poker. Players favour a style known as 'No Fold 'em Hold 'em'. Here is a typical example, witnessed by a friend of mine. Sitting next to the big blind in the $3-$6 game, he found **A♠-K♠** in the hole and raised the $3 opener to $6. All the other eight players saw his bet. My friend was not displeased with the flop, which came down **A♥-10♥-2♣**.

Everyone checked around to him, and he duly bet the regulation $3. Seemingly automatically, they all called. The turn card was the **6♥** which did not delight him. Again everyone checked around and he bet $6. And again, everybody called.

Finally on the river came the **9♥**, which was very bad news. Yet again the whole table checked. With four hearts staring him in the face, my friend could hardly risk a further bet. "Turn 'em up," ordered the dealer. Everyone showed down their hands. They were **Q-8, 8-4, J-5, 7-4, K-3, J-7, 9-5, Q-6** – all off-suit, with not a single heart among them! It is very rare to see nine hands showed down at Hold 'em, with not a properly playable hand among them. Except for the Q-6 after the turn, they were all drawing absolutely dead. My friend, dazed, raked in a $135 pot. That's No Fold 'em Hold 'em, mister!

In the higher stakes games, the standard is of course commensurately higher, but still loose. The explanation is partly inexperience among the locals and partly that the Asian players, who predominate, simply love to gamble. Be careful, however – the casinos round L.A. can be dangerous places. You should never stray outside the well-lit front entrances, and always use valet parking to collect your car (at $1 a go best value in America). One night recently another friend of mine was attacked by two armed robbers and shot in the head. Fortunately he has a tough cranium. He survived to tell the tale.

Which reminds me that *Casino*, the video, is now on sale. Its picture of Las Vegas in the corrupt 1970s is brutally accurate, if you want to see the Mafia overplaying its hand.

70

Wizardry

Why do the Americans play better than the Brits? I have been trying to find out. To point up the answer, here is a typical example of imaginative play, from the recent no limit European Hold 'em championship at the Grosvenor Victoria, when by common consent the yanks out-played the local yokels.

Freddy Deeb, a professional from Los Angeles, made a pre-flop raise of 3,000 chips in first seat after the button. Fold, fold, fold all the way round to Bobby Hough, another Vegas pro known as 'the wizard', sitting on the button. He called. Down came the flop:

7♣-7♥-Q♠

Deeb checked and Hough bet 14,000 chips. What was significant was that his bet represented well over half his remaining stack, it was not just a 'feeler' bet. Deeb who had close to 40,000 chips raised him back. The Wizard smiled. "I don't think I can beat that," he observed. He turned over a 2-3 off-suit! Deeb had checked raised with A♠-7♠.

Although this move went wrong for Hough, it was a neat play which deserved to win, and probably would win 19 times out of 20. It illustrates how the American players are always trying to build up their stacks and take control of the table.

Typically, British players' approach is to conserve their chips, run as few risks as possible, and wait for pocket aces or kings. The only trouble is that there are not enough high pairs dealt to make such a strategy viable. The Americans have years more experience under their belts, but their superiority is much richer than that. It stems from a readiness to take players on, knowing that in purely mathematical terms they may have the worst of it. They are zigging and zagging all the way through a tournament. If they get ahead, they try to get more ahead, never to sit back and coast.

Summing up the poker festival, Vegas world champion Dan Harrington was generous. "You have a few quite competent players around, but I do not think you have any players with real poker imagination." Players that is, who know all the moves and have inspiration as well as technique at their finger tips. "Maybe," Harrington conceded generously, "you Brits are better than we are at Omaha."

71

Poker on the Net

I played poker on the internet this week. An interesting experience. I did it at the city office of a poker playing friend, who occasionally lightens his business duties with an interlude of virtual poker. The game was run by an outfit called Planet Poker *(www.planetpoker.com)*.

Len, my host, had previously registered his name and credit card details with Planet Online Services. This company was run from Duluth, Georgia, but the poker was played in Costa Rica because, as everyone knows, gambling across state lines in the United States is illegal.

So after Len logged on, a picture of the outside of a casino cardroom came up on the screen. The doors opened and there we were – inside the cardroom with none of the problems of driving in and parking and waiting for a seat. It was now 12 noon on a sunny London morning, four am. in California.

Five players were engaged in a game of Hold 'em. Len knew one or two of their names from previous games – 'knew them', that is, by their style of play. The game was $3–$6 limit-raises, played quite fast, as you would expect from electronic simulation of the deal and betting. After each hand, the result was given and the player's running total of wins or losses was shown.

Planet Poker as operators raked 5% of each pot, kicking in at $1 for a $20 pot, increasing to $2 when the pot size reached $40 and capping at $3 for pots over

$60, just like in a regular casino. But it took no part in the game as such.

For my first trial at poker on the net, I put $200 (of Len's money) on the table. There were five other players in the game, from California, and one from Istanbul. First hand, when I had to post, ie. put up the blind of $3, I found (7-7) in the hole and got three callers. The other players' action was all very clearly shown on screen. I lost. Before each deal, the noise of a shuffle was played out, replicating 'real' poker. After fifteen hands, I found myself down $28.

Then I found **Ac-Qc** in the hole and raised, just one caller. The flop was no help, I bet again, and then again on fourth street. On the river a three came down, pairing the turn card. I would have checked but Len egged me on to give it a shot. I bet the $6 and my opponent folded. Hey! I was one dollar ahead.

I signed off to go to lunch. I found the experience of playing on the net quite amusing. It seems tailor-made for people who are cut-off from a proper card game. At these stakes, the downside risk is very low, and you might even win a little.

Omaha

Trouble Hand

W hen you catch a 'trouble' hand, you need to be
especially aware of danger. A trouble hand is one
that looks good, that usually wins, but has a high downside risk if it goes wrong. Donnocha O'Dea, who is one
of the most experienced players on the circuit, ran into a
typical trouble hand the other night: second best trips at
Omaha (the four card version of Texas Hold 'em).

When you flop second best 'set' (three of kind) at
Omaha you feel excited, but very nervous. The danger of
someone else flopping top set is obvious. This particular hand proved tricky because, as it turned out, three
players flopped a set.

Tony: (3-3-x-x)
Rick: (J-J-x-x)
Flop: J 8 3
Donn: (8-8-x-x)

First player to speak was Tony who bet the pot,
£200. Next player, who was the early raiser in the hand,
dropped, and it came round to Rick, who raised it by
£600. One thing Donn knew about Rick's style of play
was that he liked to hold back on good hands, in order to
check-raise. So why would he raise £600 if he held
three jacks? Rick's bet implied a holding like top two
pairs, where he wanted to drive out hands drawing to
make a straight.

Donn was certainly not going to fold his trip 8s at

that stage. He could either flat call, and hope the hand fizzled out, as often happens at Omaha if flush or straight cards appear on board; or play the man and raise him back. Donn pondered a long time over which way to go. His instinct was to play safe. But Rick's raise indicated that he did not hold three jacks. So Donn re-raised £2,400, which was all his remaining chips. Tony, who had not much money left anyway, called for about £1,200.

Rick of course stuck his money in with alacrity. The next two up-cards failed to change anything and three jacks won a nice pot.

Afterwards, Donn was rueful. If he had merely called Rick's raise of £600, he would have got away from his trouble hand. Tony, on short money, holding trip 3s, would have re-raised, and Donn would then have folded, at minimum cost. So why had Rick not checked his top set on the flop, in his usual style? He had been running badly and did not want to risk giving the others 'free' cards. Donn was right, but wrong.

73

Omaha Winner

It's never been busier or more frenetic at the World Series of Poker than it is this year. Binion's Horseshoe, that glittery garish saloon downtown, with its come as y'are, cowboy, and bet-ya boots style, is jumping. A record field is contesting the no-limit Hold 'em World Championship this week. The action, literally, never stops. Even at 6 am., 10 or 12 games are still sleepwalking through the graveyard shift.

I was glad that Donnacha o'Dea, the Irish player and one of the most popular all-round poker players in London, raised the European flag so high early on. He won the pot-limit Omaha championship, with a first prize of $154,800. He is one of the best players on the circuit but does not usually bother with tournaments. Anyway, Donnacha defeated 182 competitors, including the great Johnny Chan in a two-and-a-half hours heads-up final. Chan tops the roster of all-time world series money winners with tournament earnings of $2.3m.

The crucial hand saw Donnacha with K-J-5-3 flop a wheel (A-2-3-4-5) while Chan (known as the Orient Express) flopped a set of 4s.The straight held up and in the next hand Donn finished him off by catching four 8s. British player Steve Rydell, a former jeweller from Stoke-on-Trent, finished a creditable fifth, winning $17,415.

Some people believe that the Europeans play Omaha better than the Americans, who are superior at Hold 'em. Maybe so, maybe not. The real distinction is probably between pot limit poker, where the British are far more experienced, and limit play, which is the style the Americans are used to. Anyway, the old country is not doing too badly at Hold 'em either. The last three in a field of 172 in the pot-limit event were all our boys.

Steve Rydell on this, his first visit to the World Series, led all the way at the final table to take first place, with a prize of $104,600. Dave 'Devil Fish' Ulliott from Hull was second. "I started the final table in lowest chip position and played my socks off," he declared. Surindar Sunar of Wolverhampton, probably the most consistent tournament player in England, came third.

You want to know how I'm doing myself, don't you? Well, I have managed to win enough in the cash games to pay for my satellite entries. In the super-satellite I played, which cost only $220 to enter, I lasted all of 15 minutes. The finalists all won their $10,000 entry fee into the World Championship. But you won't get any hard luck stories from me. The week is still young!

74

No Split

The pot was worth $30,000 so a lot of people were surprised I didn't take the offer to split it," said Stewart. "But why should I split when I thought I was best?" The game was Omaha, the four card version of Texas Hold 'em. What was surprising to the other players in the game was that Stewart only had two pairs 8s and 2s, with one card to come, and his opponent almost certainly had a pair of aces.

Here's how it went. First man to speak raised the opening bet and Stewart in next seat called with a rather moderate hand, A-8-4-2. (His A-8 were suited, but that is not relevant to the story.) Three other players called. The flop came out 8-7-2. Now the raiser bet again. What has he got? Raising in first position, Stewart put him on a pair of aces, trying to buy the pot. So he called, fearing the others could be winning. But they dropped. Fourth flop card was a 3, no help. Stewart bet again, the raiser called and immediately offered to spit the pot.

Stewart: A 8 4 2
Flop: 8 7 2 3

Splitting pots or 'doing deals' is quite common in Las Vegas, as I have reported before. But there is another way of doing it, which is to divide the pot into two, and then deal out a 5th up-card, and then separately a 6th up-card, to decide each half of the pot, independently. It is a way of spreading the risk. If the man had a pair of aces in the hole, there were only 8 cards left to help him. (He can make aces-ups if a 7 or a 3 comes on board, or trip aces with another ace. An 8 or a 2 gives Stewart a full house). So not surprisingly, Stewart won. He had read the aces correctly.

The obvious question was why, if he was such a red hot favourite, should Stewart offer to deal out the extra card? His explanation is that poker is a social game. It is important that the players round the table feel happy, especially the losers. This applies to fun games played around the kitchen table as well as in high stakes professional games, as this was. If he had offered to split the pot, Stewart would have given up his whole advantage of his good play. By offering to deal out the extra cards, for each half of the pot, he preserved his mathematical advantage (as he would have done if every single card remaining in the deck had been dealt) and at the same time gave his opponent an 'out', which he was glad to take.

75

Blockers

Blockers, or cards which block your opponent, are a tempting concept at Omaha (the four card version of Hold 'em). If for example, the first three cards of the flop show 9-10-Q, and you happen to hold a couple of jacks in your hand, the chance of your opponent also holding a jack to make a straight is greatly reduced.

From that premise, it follows that you do not need to have an 8 or a king in your hand, to go with one of your jacks (in Omaha you have to play two cards from your hand). You can bet as if you had made a straight, on the presumption that your jacks block your opponent. He won't be able to call a big bet, if he just has top pair, or even two pairs.

The concept is a good one, but it can come unstuck, as was demonstrated in the final of the Omaha tournament at the Victoria the other night. 54 players were competing for a total prize of £42,500. After several hours play it came down to Surinder Sunar from Wolverhampton, who is the most successful tournament player in the country, and a lively Irish player, Chris Dalton. At one stage he had twice as many chips as Sunar and looked likely to scoop first prize.

On what turned out to be the final hand, Chris made a fair sized bet before the flop, holding 6-7-J-J – not a great hand but at heads-up, a fair start. Surinder called. The final was very tense, with one or the other player escaping what looked like sudden death on all-in bets several times.

Out came the flop:

9-10-Q

Now Chris's two jacks are the blockers. It looked an ideal moment to win a good sized pot. So he stuck his money in. Surinder, as is his style, paused a moment. As luck would have it, he also had a jack.

He held 5-7-8-J, which made him a straight, but only the lower straight. If Chris had J-K he was winning. Surinder did not hesitate for long. He stood up and pushed his chips forward. The players turned their hands over. Chris's other two cards gave him no 'outs'.

It is easy, from the outside, to criticize his play as too speculative. But against a player of Sunar's talent, it is no use just sitting still.

"I had the blockers," lamented Chris, "the only trouble is there are four jacks in the deck." Second prize of £10,000 was some consolation. "I did not like putting my money in on the low end straight," was Sunar's response. "But at that stage I had no choice."

76

Crazy or Cute?

Crazy or inspired? Here's a conundrum from Omaha. On the flop, you really need to have the 'nuts' or be drawing to the 'nuts'. In high stakes games any other strategy is too risky, but the equation can be very complicated. This example comes from the big game at the Grosvenor Victoria.

Mr. Clever Clogs was dealt 8♣ 7♣ 6♦ 3♣ and called the initial £25 bet. Mr. Wild to his immediate left raised the pot, Mr. Cautious and Mr. Erratic both called. C-C called along. The pot now stood at £700. The flop came down 9♦ 5♦ 2♠.

Mr. Erratic now came out betting £700. C-C saw he would make the nut straight with an 8,7,6 or 4 provided none were diamonds (allowing a diamond flush). So he had 10 nut outs and would likely be paid off he hit any of them. He called. Mr. Wild called and raised £150 'all in' (no more chips left). Mr. Cautious and Mr. Erratic both called as did C-C. Presumably one player had trips and another a diamond flush draw, and the third a straight draw (which might split the pot with C-C). £4,100 in the pot.

The next card brought a 10♥. Mr. Erratic went all in for £2,500. Now C-C went into a long think. Mr. Cautious had only £1,000 left. So if C-C won the pot he would receive £7,600. Was it worth wagering £2,500 for this?

The true answer could be determined only after the last card came down and all the players' holdings were revealed. Mr. Erratic had 9♠ 9♣ A 3♦, Mr. Cautious held A♦ K♥ J♦ 8♠, Mr. Wild K♦ K♣ 5♣ 2♦ (he had bundled his money in hoping for a third king). Given all this, Mr. C-C would win with a jack (3 cards), 8 (2), 6 (3), or 4 (3). In addition, if a 7 came down he would win £1,500 from Mr. Erratic but lose the main pot to Mr. Cautious. Thus he had 11 outs from 32 cards remaining, approximately 2-1. In fact a 4 came down and he won £7,600 for his £2,500 wager, 3-1. Crazy or cute?

77

Folding the Nuts

One of the trickiest decisions in poker is folding the best hand. It happened to me in a round of Omaha at the Stakis Regency in Russell Square (where the poker continues to flourish Mondays through Fridays) the other night. I called a raise on 9-7-5-4, and the flop came down 10♠-8♠-6♥, giving me a nice straight – at that point the nuts. Two very strong players ahead of me.

Player A now bet the pot, £65 and B followed. My first thought was to raise. The trouble is my hand is completely lifeless. Sure, it's best at the moment (more likely equal best) but it cannot improve. Two spades on the board point to a possible flush draw. And if a jack or a queen falls and someone happens to have Q-9 or J-9, my straight may be useless. I called to see what would happen, feeling actually that the smart move might be to fold!

Down came a 5♥ – so far so good, no improvement for anyone. Now to my surprise Player A bet the pot, £260, all-in. As he knew either B or myself or possibly both of us had straights, he obviously had to have a premium hand himself, perhaps a double flush draw now that a second heart had come down. If so, this gave him odds of about 2-1 to hit, against 3-1 in the pot, if both his opponents called the bet.

Player B then went all-in himself for a shade more, £300, clearly intending to drive me out. I looked at my cards again. There was no way my straight could improve. Even if it held up I would win only half the pot, or perhaps just a third. Reluctantly I folded the nuts. The last card was a deuce and B won the pot on a 10-high straight. He also had two pairs 8s and 6s, which was valuable back-up for a full house draw.

A day or two later, when people are relaxed about previous clashes at the table, I asked A what he had. He told me Q-J to give him a higher straight if the missing 9 came down, and also two 10s for top trips. "I thought I was favourite to win the hand," he told me. "But when you folded, the money odds were only 2-1. Perhaps I should have checked on the turn (fourth card), and let B bet it. You would probably have called and I would have had better value." This was a typical Omaha situation, when you have to measure fluctuations in odds against your knowledge of the players.

7 Card Stud

78

Lucky Strike

Des got lucky in a hand of seven card stud, but he also played it well.

In that sense he 'made' his luck. He was dealt **(9-9) 8** in his hand, and called the man to his right, a predictable old club player, who opened £1 on his ace showing. On his left a weak player, who was having a lucky run, called on a queen. But Paddy, a gambling sort of punter in last seat, who had just breezed in from Dublin, raised a fiver, showing a jack. The other three called.

It is hard to hit trips – the odds of catching another 9 at that point are over 20-1 – but Des' pair was concealed. And he was lucky enough to catch his third 9, while looking like a straight draw.

A: (?-?) A♣-Q♥
Des: (9-9) 8♣-9♠
C: (? ?) Q♦-10♥
Paddy: (? ?) J♠-A♠

When player A, first to act, bet £20 he was as good as declaring a pair of aces. If he had trips he would check. Des knew if he raised, he would very likely win a small pot, without more ado. Many players prefer to do this, rather than risk being outdrawn. But he just called the £20. Player C who might be straightening or have a pair of queens, called. And now Paddy socked it right back by calling the £20 and raising another £80, all-in, on his two spades. It was pretty obvious, knowing him, that he was gambling on a four flush.

Player A did not like this at all. He havered and wavered, because he knew what Paddy was up to, but he finally called the £80.

Joy for Des! He called the £80 and re-raised £200. Player C thought about it and folded. Paddy was all-in. Player A – this was the point – could not call on his pair of aces, especially as another ace was out. He had stuck in £100 without even being able to see the hand through.

Des was now a big favourite against Paddy's four flush. Paddy indeed hit a spade, but Des paired up for a house, and won a £250 pot at minimal risk. Though aggression is the key to poker, restraint sometimes pays better.

79

Winning Error

Everyone makes mistakes at poker. The worst thing, after making a mistake, is to brood about it hand after hand, which simply compounds the original error, and makes you play even worse. Once it's happened it's over, like a shot missed at golf. I am very prone to dream about mistakes for a days on end, even if I've won the pot, which is doubly foolish.

In a lively seven card stud game the other night, I was first to speak on **A (A K)**, obviously a big starting hand. A good player on my right called showing a **7**, following a mercurial type opposite on a **10**. Fourth street was blank but fifth street gave me an ace for trip aces. The player to my right caught another **7** and the player opposite a second deuce showing. I thought the hand was all over. They could see I was high, and knew I played tight. But they both called. Then on 6th street the hands got really interesting. I caught a king for a concealed full house aces and kings, but my opponents each made open trips.

A: (x x) 7 4 7 7
B: (A-K) A 9 A K
C: (x x) 10 2 2 2

How to play this? After it was all over, I decided the correct play was to raise it up and face the consequences. I had about £300 to risk, and if I ran into four of a kind, that was too bad. But when the trip 7s player bet a mere £25 I started havering. His 'door card' or first card up was a 7, so it was quite likely he started with a 7 in the hole.

Was he betting small to lure me in?

So I just flat-called the £25, giving the impression (very bad play) of extreme nervousness. Player C at once jumped in with a huge raise. I wasn't really worried about him because his door card was not a 2, and it was difficult to envisage any starting hand for him which included a 2 in the hole. The trip 7s player now called the raise and with so much money at stake, I stuck the rest of my chips in. It turned out they both had low full houses. My hesitant play, though quite wrong, served to build a huge pot. I did not feel pleased with myself, despite winning.

(80)

Outdraw

I f there were no out-draws at poker, there would be no betting. The best hand at the start would always win. I was reminded of this truth by a lucky outdraw at seven card study at the Victoria casino the other night. On fourth street Spiro, a strong gambler, not afraid of putting his money where his mouth is, showed a **Q-J** offsuit. The pot had already been well bet on the first two rounds. Spiro now re-raised £220.

It's obvious enough he has a high pair, if not two pairs. What is more, everyone understood that there was no way, short of a crow-bar across the knuckles, of dissuading him from seeing this hand through to the death. That is the kind of guy Spiro is.

But Derry, sitting on a pathetic looking ♦5-♦9, now called the £220 and re-raised £660 all in. I thought he must have concealed trips because three diamonds were out, including a hand showing ♦A-♦8, which now folded. It's certainly a very bad play to bet so much money to hit a flush, when several cards of your suit are out. Even if Derry has a higher card in the hole than Spiro, say a Kd, it's a pretty faint hope to catch a higher pair to save himself, if his four-flush does not fill.

But Derry had obviously failed to read *Seven Card Stud for Advanced Players*, which warns: "If three of your suit are out, your three flush is just about always unplayable."

Spiro: (9♥ Q♠) Q♠ J♣
Derry: (7♦ 2♦) 5♦ 9♦

Derry's re-raise would probably have persuaded me to fold, admittedly. I would not want to gamble all my chips on a single pair of queens standing up, even if I am an 11-10 favourite. (The advantage is too narrow for the cost). But Spiro, true to form, barely hesitated. For him, a high pair is p-o-w-e-r.

"Trips?" inquired Spiro as the dealer stacked up the chips. "I'm only going for the flush," Derry confessed. The next two cards off were blanks, but on seventh street he hit the elusive diamond, 10-high. The pot was worth nearly £2,000. I was surprised at his play because Derry is a pro, in the sense that he doesn't do much else but play cards. So later I asked him why he stuck so much money in on such a bad bet. I thought his answer compounded his misplay.

"Sure and I'd won a grand in a previous game, so I decided I might as well gamble it," he explained.

(81)

Putting it Down

Some hands you just can't get away from, which is very annoying. I'm thinking of situations at seven card stud where you start off with a high concealed pair such as (Q–Q) in the hole and raise the pot, in order to induce hands with a higher door card showing, such as an ace or a king, to fold. The idea is to cut down the field to a single opponent, when your high pair is a good favourite to stand up. If you both catch nondescript cards on fourth street, you bet again; likewise on fifth street. In this instance, my opponent got no help on fifth street, whereas I caught an ace.

A: (Q♣-Q♦) 7♥ 10♦ A♣
B: (?-?) 8♥ 2♦ 5♣

Player A simply has to bet the pot. If he merely checks, he gives B a free draw, to whatever he may or may not have in the hole. B, after all, has no flush or straight draw showing. If he had aces or kings wired in the hole, he would surely have re-raised on the first round.

The fifth card at seven card stud is a turning point. In this instance, I bet the pot, which was about £65. My opponent raised £150. He must have something down there, dammit! Probably just two small pairs, if he came in with say 8 (8–5). This is a miserable starting hand, but player B, who was a bit of a gambler, might well have tried it. One ace had already gone, so he probably read my hand for a medium pair, and was taking a chance to drive me out, for the money. I didn't put him on trips 8s, though he could have caught a lucky 5 to a concealed pair of 5s.

We both had another couple of hundred in chips, which he would know I would not want to commit on a lone pair. So I folded. My side cards were live, but the price was too high.

A few days later I asked B what he had. "I had you beat," he told me. Poker players, notoriously, seldom tell the truth so I still don't know whether to believe him.

(82)

Three Queens

Three queens showed on the opening round of a game of seven card stud at the Grosvenor Victoria casino. The first queen was obliged to bring it in with an opening bet of £1. The other two queen hands folded. There were low cards out around the board. I looked down and found **(6-7) 8** in my hand, and called. Next card off gave the opener, Ali, who was a shrewd player, with a sizeable stack of chips in front of him, a second queen. I caught an **8** for a pair of 8s showing. He bet £10 at me, all the low card hands folded, so I raised him £30, representing trip 8s.

To my annoyance, not to say surprise, Ali called me. Doesn't everyone know I'm harder to crack than granite? I knew Ali couldn't have three queens, of course. But what I overlooked was an important principle of poker. *He knew I knew!* He read my raise as exploiting my knowledge and interpreted it, correctly, as a steal. It is extremly important in poker to take account of what your opponent thinks you think, not just what you think he thinks.

Fifth street game me a jack and Ali a 10. If I was going to make him put his hand down it was now or never. So I bet £90 at him. He called without a flicker. So much for my representing trip 8s. He probably had a low pair in the hole to go with his queens. I could still catch two cards to hit a miracle straight, but the jig was up. So I checked and failed to improve.

Ali checked after the last down card. I pondered

momentarily whether to take one more shot at it, by betting the pot at him. But he obviously had two pairs minimum, maybe a top straight, and would certainly have called me. I threw away my hand rather than exposing the ignominy of my bluff.

"Very generous!" Ali observed, raking in the chips.

"I knew you had trip 8s beaten," I countered feebly.

"Would you like to know what I had?" he asked.

"No, I would not!"

But Ali was not to be deterred so easily. "Three queens!" he announced. I ground my teeth.

83

Intuition

"**I** knew I should have called that hand!" Jack swore. It was seven card stud and a player across the table had bluffed the pot on an open pair against Jack's higher concealed pair. "Always trust your intuition!" he wailed. Was he right? Yes, mostly. Intuition at poker and other games is not the same thing as pre-cognition. Contrary to what many gamblers feel, there is no rational basis for pre-cognition, the idea that you can somehow sense what number is going to come up on the next roll. My own problem with roulette, for instance, is that I do not prefer one number over any other.

Intuition at cards is different. It is an instinctive mental process based on pattern recognition. It happens when a player picks up a signal of some sort – word or gesture or movement from an opponent – which tells him something is going on, beyond his ordinary conscious perception of the play. A parallel in football is the 'reflex save' by a goalkeeper when, somehow, he gets to a shot which seems to defy the laws of gravity.

In a high-low game the other night, which we jokingly call 'Terror Without Mercy' (five cards in hand, plus eight cards dealt face-up in common!) I made a perfect low **6-4-3-2-A** and also a low full house. One opponent kept calling. I sensed, in a way I could not put into words, that he wanted to play the hand to the end, that he had something good down there. It was a perfectly valid intuition, deduced from his manner or voice or whatever. I should simply have declared low for half the pot, but I got greedy and went both ways. He had a higher full house, which scooped the whole pot.

When a player makes a heavy bet, another player will often sit and ponder. He is not thinking so much about his own hand as the behaviour of the bettor. In the pause, as the table falls silent, a sensitive player can sometimes pick up a tremor, an emanation of fear or of confidence, which can be crucial. Such a signal may be misread. But as a rule it is a good idea to trust these not quite extra-sensory perceptions.

84

Slow Playing

Have you noticed how many players repeat their mistakes? I can think of a myriad players who can be relied on to over-bet two high pairs at seven stud, or bluff-raise a four flush draw at Hold 'em, or pump a pair aces at Omaha as if they were hooked to a life support machine.

A basic error which many novice players commit is to slow-play (under-bet) a strong hand. This simply gives their opponents the gift of 'free' cards to draw out on them. Here is a recent case.

Reg, who evidently fancied himself as a seven card stud player, found trip deuces on fourth street, and set out to tempt Igor, who everyone knew was a terrible player.

Reg: (A♦-2♣) 2♥ 2♠
Igor: (? ?) 10♣ 7♦

Reg checked and Igor bet the pot, £7. Reg ever so reluctantly called. To me, his trip deuces were flashing like the lights in Picadilly Circus, but no matter. On fifth street, no visible improvement to either hand. Igor chose to bet £20, and Reg again made a slow call, luring his opponent on, whereas a re-raise at this point was mandatory. On sixth street, the same pattern was repeated, with £60 bets. It was obvious that Igor was pulling to a straight draw and Reg was hoping to turn his trips into a full house – which he failed to do.

But now, after the last card had been dealt in the hole, Reg waded in with a pot-sized bet of £180. This was the worst possible moment to bet. Igor (even he) will call only if he has made his hand. Which he duly did. If Reg had been trying to lose his money on purpose he could not have played it worse.

Whereas he would probably have won the pot, albeit a small one, then and there if he had bet his trips on fourth, or certainly fifth street, as he should have done. If Igor chose to call, as knowing him he might have, he would have had to pay for the privilege of drawing out.

Moral: slow play your hand only if you are sure your opponent has virtually no chance of improving; or ideally, your hand is so strong you do not fear any kind of outdraw.

High Low

85

Biggest Game In Town

The biggest game around, open to all-comers, is probably in London. No doubt far bigger games are spread in Las Vegas periodically; and higher stakes private games may be held among friends. But as a regular game, the Omaha/London lowball game at the Victoria Casino in the Edgware Road, consisting of alternate rounds of Omaha (the four card version of Texas Hold 'em) and London low-ball (6-4 low) is where it's at, three days a week.

The buy-in is £1,000 which may seem manageable; in practice it means a player needs to feel comfortable sitting down with at least three or four grand and be prepared to bring up more if needed, and more again.

I asked Stewart Reuben, one of the regulars, what has kept the game going for four years. His explanation is that because there are smaller games at the Vic, where you can sit down with as little as £50, it creates a pyramid of players, who can move up from one game to another at higher stakes.

The two kinds of game chosen for the big table make an intriguing contrast: Omaha is a sophisticated, complex, card-reading game; seven card lowball is a deceptively simple, strong betting game. In tandem they provide a good test of skill and nerve.

Here is an example of a recent Omaha hand, which stunned the table.

Ted: A♥ J♣ 6♥ 2♠

Flop: Q♥ 8♥ 6♦ 2♣ -
Joe: K♥ 10♥ 6♣ 2♦

At Omaha, each player must use two cards from his hand, combined with three from the five flop cards, dealt face up in common. Somehow or other, Ted and Joe, neither having managed to make anything more than the two bottom pairs, 6s and 2s, contrived to goad each other into sticking £8,000 into the pot. No money left to bet, one final flop card to come.

Joe has a terrible hand, with no "nut" (absolute best) card to draw to; Ted's hand is scarcely better, but at least a heart will give him nut flush. Out came the last card on the river, 8♣.

Both players turned over their dismally poor holdings and everyone gazed in awe at so much money being spent on such garbage. Everyone agreed they split the pot, including the dealer (whose duty it is to call the best hand). Finally someone noticed that the best hand was not 6s and 2s, after all. Ted has A-6 in his hand to make 8s and 6s with an ace. Joe's best hand is 8s and 6s with a king.

Ted expressed surprise that Stewart had not not spotted this. Why hadn't Ted noticed it for himself? His excuse was he had imbibed rather too well shortly before the game. Heigh-ho.

86

High Low Dilemma

It's painful, but sometime you have to fold when you have the best hand. I am thinking particularly of high-low games, when the cost of the hand going wrong, even though you are best, makes it too risky and to expensive to play it out.

Here's a recent example from Omaha high-low. (In this game players have four cards in the hand, from which they must use any two, in combination with three from the five flop cards). On the flop, Mel made three jacks, which was clearly the best high hand at that point: and there was no low hand as yet, because in this game the low had to be 8 or better to qualify.

Flop: 4♣ 5♣ J♥
Mel: (J J K 10)

Mel bet £15 but when Stan, the only other player in, called and raised £45, Mel is in trouble. His three jacks are best, no doubt about that. And there may never be an 8-low, if the last two flop cards are high. But the question is: what has Stan got?

It's pretty obvious, if you know anything about high-low. Stan has got a flush draw to the Ace-x of clubs, which means that any club which falls will give him best high: and he also holds four cards to a low hand – probably A-2 – so another low card on board will give him a winning low. A bonus with this kind of holding is that a low card, such as a 3, will also give him a low straight, to win the high as well. His hand, therefore, will probably look something like:

Stan: A♣ Q♣ 2♦ 6♥

Now if Mel calls the raise (as he did) he faces a £135 bet on the fourth card (which he also called), and £400 on the river. Although his three jacks was still best hand, he can never win the low. He might well improve to a full house if one of the flop cards pairs up, but his opponent will certainly not call him if it does. He is therefore sticking in his money, and quite a lot of it, simply to try and win half the pot, ie. get his own money back again.

This is bad value. Mel managed to fold, and regretted calling the previous bets. It is simply too expensive to go on with this kind of hand.

A lot of players will fall in love with a good high hand like trips, or by the same token, four low cards. But against a single opponent, when you stand to win only half the pot, that is a recipe for disaster. A multiway pot, which offers some value if you split it, is a different matter.

(87)

Inventor's Coup

Inventor Sir Clive Sinclair is never happier than at his drawing board, devising some new wheeze like his ZETA motor for bicycles. This useful device saves pedalling uphill – a feat he has plenty of experience at in high-low poker. Going downhill, however, all you need to do is apply the brakes at the right moment. Sir Clive gave a good demonstration of this technique the other night, playing five card Omaha (8 or better for low), when he found A♣-K♣-K♥-7♣-5♥ in his hand and the flop came down K♦-K♠-6♣.

The main aim in this dream situation, obviously, is to pick up speed without driving the other players out of the race. This means checking along and not taking over the betting. But the second aim, when playing high-low, is to try and make it a one way hand, so that the high hand wins the whole pot. If someone makes a low hand, he may back in for half the pot, which more or less wipes out the value of the high hand.

So Clive, first to speak, checked. No one had raised the blinds before the flop and no one ventured a bet now. Everyone was very leery of trip kings. On fourth street, a low card came down, a 4♣. Now the situation changed. Someone holding the ace of clubs may be tempted to draw to a flush, or with two pairs go for a full house. On the low side it is not, as a general rule, a good idea to call a big bet if you have only four cards to a low hand, even the ace-deuce. If a high card falls on fifth street, the low may never materialize, or the ace or deuce may be duplicated on board. Occasionally, if no one can raise again behind you, and half the pot is offering better than 2-1 for the money, you can risk it. A man's gotta do what a man's gotta do.

In this instance, last card was a 3♦. This was not good news for Clive. Someone has almost certainly made the nut low, to back in and snitch half the pot. Sure enough, one man bet out. There was no point in holding back any longer, so Clive check-raised. The man called. Clive showed his kings for four of a kind. The other player took a quick look at Clive's two cards A-5 for the low, and folded without showing his own hand. "Nicely played", he felicitated the inventor through gritted teeth.

(88)

Heartbreaker

Here is the hand that broke my heart in Las Vegas. I was playing Omaha high-low, which is an intriguing game because in nearly every hand you face a decision, like taking the cube in backgammon, whether to take a double or fold. In these fast-paced limit games, declaration is by showdown.

So, after struggling all day and all night, I was dealt:

A♣-2♥-3♦-J♣

which is a powerful starter. Any three cards from 3 to 8 on the flop will give me the 'nut' low and I am also drawing to a nut high flush. The game was $15–$30 raises, but this was a 'kill' hand – an adrenalin-provoking twist whereby the stakes are automatically doubled next hand, every time a player scoops the whole pot.

Naturally I raised the opener and got two callers. Down came the flop:

4♣-6♣-9♥

I raised again. Any new low card from A–2–3–5–7–8 gives me the nut low. When a high club came on the turn, my anticipation of joy was unconfined.

Now I had the nut flush made, in case someone was straightening. I was a huge favourite to scoop and virtually certain to take half, if not three quarters of the pot (should another player share the low).

So I upped it again. Two of the remaining three players immediately folded. But on the river, down came another 6, making a low pair on the board. My remaining opponent lit up like the neon sign outside the casino and bet another $60 at me.

I knew I was beaten, but what can you do? There is just too much in the pot to let it go. He had hit a low full house.

I did not go mad. Nor did I go on tilt. I got up and went to lunch, or whatever passes for lunch at five in the morning, and swigged down a bottle of red wine. Then I went to bed.

89

Nowt

A variation of poker that seems to attract mistakes like
summer wasps is Omaha high-low, which is currently
enjoying a revival at the Stakis Regency in Russell
Square, London WC1. Instead of a declaration high or
low (which of course in home games provides most of
the fun), hands are shown down to the dealer.

The best way to make money is to win both ways. A
lock on the low side is not too difficult, especially if you
start with a hand like A-2, or better A-2-3. All you need
then is three low cards on the flop which do not dupli-
cate your own hand. The danger is that someone else
will have the same holding, so your half is split, and you
win only a quarter of the pot, or in a three-way tie only a
sixth.

Sometimes it is prudent to fold such a hand, even
with a lock. Here is a case in point.

B: ♠A-♣2-♥6-♦K
Flop: ♦Q ♠8 ♥4

Four players in the hand, one raise before the flop,
checked all around on the flop. Next card ♦7. Now
player B, second to speak, has a nut low, with one card
to come. Everyone has two or three hundred pounds in
front of them.

A, the player to B's right, first to speak, bet the pot:
£30. It looks as if he has made a straight. Should B raise
his lock low? The best he can hope for is to knock the

others out and take half the pot; the risk is that someone will re-raise and he will be squeezed, out-drawn and quartered. So B merely called.

Player C then raised £75 and D re-raised £150. Player A called without hesitation. Now B is in trouble. His hand is lifeless. Someone has certainly got a lock low with him, and if the river card brings an ace or a deuce, duplicating his low cards, he will very likely be out-gunned by an A-3 or 2-3.

It is tough to put down a lock low, but in that situation, with no realistic hope of backing in for the high half (such as a straight or flush draw), I think it is the right play.

Player B disagreed and put all his money in. A deuce of diamonds came on the river, giving one man a flush and another a nut 7 low. In a £1,060 split pot, B got back nowt.

90

Silly Me

Oone of the commonest mistakes you can make at poker, or more accurately which I make, is to get a single hand out of proportion to the rest of the game. The other night, having turned a hefty loss into a moderate win at Omaha high-low, I was feeling rather pleased with myself.

A final hand was agreed. I was dealt **10-J-J-K**, which is promising enough. There was a raise before the flop, which came down **6-7-J** off-suit. A fearless gambler on my right took a wild re-raise after the initial round of betting, which made it £150 to go.

My first instinct was to raise him back because, after all, I had the best high at that stage with trip jacks. What's more, if no other low cards came on the board (to qualify, the low hand has to be 8 or better), it would be a one-way pot. My second instinct was to fold, despite having the best hand. Why get involved at this late hour against a big gambler? But prompted by a mocking internal voice inquiring 'Are you a man or a mouse?' I called the bet. Two other players were already all-in. Next card off was a 9. My opponent checked. It was obvious he had not hit a straight.

A (**10-J-J-K**)
Flop **6-7-J-9**
B (**x-x-x-x**)

A low hand was now unlikely though not quite out

of the question if he was hoping to back in for half the pot. I checked along, because I knew if I bet, even with the top trips, he would call, against the odds, especially if he also had a straight draw like a 4-5. I did not want to over-play my own hand.

Last card was another 7, giving me best full house, jacks on sevens. He paused and then bet £300 at me. If he had started with a pair of 7s, hitting the case 7 was a 43-1 shot. These things do happen. But on the chance that he only had a full house 6s, or more likely, knowing him, that he was trying to bomb me out, I called. He showed me four 7s and I retired with a sore head.

I should never have got involved on this hand, which was way out of line with the rest of the game. I got it back later in the week but that did not console me for my poor judgement. If you are going to make a mistake at poker, it is cheaper to do it by folding rather than calling.

91

London Lowball

S even card stud low-ball is such a simple game on the surface. But it is ruthless in its demands. Here is a case in point from the big game at the Victoria club in London. The best low hand is A-2-3-4-6, off-suit (as distinct from wheel A-2-3-4-5 as played in America).

Antes were £10 a player, with high card showing forced to 'bring it in', or make the first bet, which in this game was a hefty £25. Stewart called on **(8-2) A**, all the other players showing high cards passed, as did one showing an 8 and two others with a deuce. Sid, who is an excitable, up-and-down kind of player, raised the pot also showing an ace. Stewart called.

Next card gave Sid a **3** and Stewart a **5**. Sid again bet the size of the pot. Nothing gives him greater pleasure than bluffing out Stewart, who is known as a shrewd competitor, and aggressive with it. But this time Sid exuded strength.

Stewart put him on (6-4) in the hole, which would give him a draw to make a perfect low. If Sid held that hand, he was clearly a 2-1 favourite. But with several thousand pounds between them, Stewart felt he had value. The only low cards to have folded were ones he held himself, so he was unlikely to pair up; and he had a good idea of his opponent's hand.

Card five brought Sid a **10** and Stewart a **Q**. Stewart knew he should probably pass. He may never make a hand better than a 10 low. At this stage it is more a matter of feel, the intuition of the moment, than maths. So he called, and was rewarded with a 9 on card 6 while Sid paired his 3s.

> Sid: (6-4) A 3 10 3
> Stewart: (A-2) 8 5 Q 9

At last Stewart had hit the front, so he set Sid in for all of his chips, a matter of £8,000. Sid called, and hit a magic 7 to win the pot.

In the post-mortem a very experienced player whispered to Stewart that he should not have played against such a hand, when his opponent had three chances after fourth street to hit a 2, 5 or 7, and leave him stranded. Other people of equally sound judgement maintained he was quite correct.

92

Crazy Bill Again

Seven card lowball is an infuriating game, but not without skill. The idea is to catch the lowest cards possible, so the best hand is A-2-3-4-6 off-suit. A 7-low is very strong, and an 8-low usually a winner. It can be very frustrating when you keep getting dealt high pairs or catch good cards to fill a low full house, but that's the game.

Weird things can happen at lowball, as this hand shows. It was played by the ever-popular Crazy Bill, a player who thinks odds are something to do with matching up different coloured socks. In this game, high card showing has to 'bring it in', by making the opening bet. After performing his reluctant duty, the high card usually drops, but not Crazy Bill.

When Louie, known as a very aggressive and clever player raised the pot, showing a 7 as his up-card, everyone else dropped. Crazy Bill took the view that having been obliged to invest £25 on his queen, he might as well call another £100 to get it back. (This was a big game). Next card up Louie caught a 4. Wild Bill got a jack. No matter. Now he called a £300 bet. On fifth street the picture changed. Louie caught another 4, to make a pair showing, Crazy Bill got a 5.

Louie (2-6) 7 4 4
Bill   (A 2) Q J 5

It is true that Crazy Bill's queen now makes him the

low hand. But even with an A-2 in the hole he is still a huge underdog with two cards to come. So Louie (who used to teach maths) bet £900 at him. Next card he was dealt an ace to make a 7-low, and breathed a sigh of relief. Crazy Bill also got a 7, but still had to draw out to win. So Louie set him in for the rest of his chips.

Naturally Wild Bill called. Louie got an 8 as his last card in the hole, but Crazy Bill pulled a magic 3, to scoop a huge pot, A-2-3-5-7 against A-2-4-6-7.

Many people curse their luck when they get outdrawn, but that is the wrong reaction. According to Louie weaker players must be made to feel loved and admired, never criticized. If they are given lessons at the table, they may learn to play better and stop making so many mistakes. On the night in question, the gods of chance were consistent. Crazy Bill still managed to go home a loser, and my friend got it back. You can buck the odds some of the time. But if you buck the odds all of the time, you will wind up without socks of any colour.

(93)

Lowball Coup

Lowball, the version of seven card stud when the best possible hand is A-2-3-4-6 off-suit, is a tricky game. Someone once told me it was merely 2% skill and 98% luck. I think it is more complicated than most players realize. It certainly can be very expensive. Here is a case in point.

In a six handed-game at the Grosvenor Victoria, no one had any low card showing. In this, the big game, everyone antes a tenner and the high card has to 'bring it in', that is make a forced opening bet, for £25. (It seems a lot but it works out much the same for everyone in the long run.) Luigi, a competent player called the opening bet on a queen and Liam, a very shrewd player, raised on his 10 showing. Ibrahim, who has a reputation on both sides of the Atlantic as a fearless gambler, called on a king showing! Now the money was such that Luigi felt he must call the raise.

On fourth street, that is the second up-card, Liam caught an 8 and bet the pot, now worth £800. Ibrahim gaily chose to call with a K-Q, which is a terrible hand! And again Luigi felt he had to call on the principle of value for money. On fifth street, all three players caught 9s. Liam bet the pot, £1,700 all-in and Ibrahim finally surrendered. What were Luigi's chances?

Luigi (A-2) Q 7 9
Liam (? ?) 10 8 9

Clearly, Luigi is looking for a 3, 4, 5 or 6 to win (an 8 is probably not good enough), that is 16 cards out of the 37 he doesn't know about. His chance of hitting on sixth or seventh street works out at about 2-1, which is what the pot is paying. So he should call. Liam may, after all, have a bad card in the hole, and be bluffing. The key to the play is that Luigi has to improve only *once*, by drawing a low card to make a 9 low; whereas if he makes it Liam would need to improve *twice*, by catching low cards on both sixth and seventh streets.

If there were a lot more money to be bet, it would be different. Luigi would have to decide, if he improves, whether Liam would fold. In the event, he caught an 8 on sixth street to nose ahead. But Liam outdrew him on the river to make a better 9-8 low and win a £5,000 pot. It is easy to get sucked into these kind of hands at lowball. It's a matter of judgement whether it's worth it.